Advance Praise for *Diagnosis: Poverty*

"Marcella Wilson is that rare person who combines intellect and humor, vision and practicality, and empathy for others. Dr. Wilson's Transition To Success model, which includes continuous quality improvement, will help build a bridge between public health and human services."

–Phil Basso, Deputy Executive Director, The American Public Human Services Association, Washington, DC

"In her warm and engaging colloquial voice, Marcella Wilson explains how coordinated care management and other best practices, coupled with volunteerism and financial literacy, evolved into the Transition To Success model for treating poverty as an environmentally based medical condition."

–Tom Page, Executive Director, Michigan 2-1-1, Lansing, MI

"Marcella Wilson uses data, statistics, and a huge dose of common sense in her efforts to get us all to rethink our view of poverty. I came to know Detroit and America better through a new set of lenses that Dr. Wilson provides. This excellent work should become a standard for people and organizations that deal with public life and provide services to those in need."

–Edward Branch, Pastor, Third New Hope Baptist Church, Detroit, MI

"This is a compelling personal narrative, with a strong application of theory to practice. Diagnosis: Poverty *challenges us to address and treat the 'condition of poverty,' perhaps one of the greatest social-justice issues of our time."*

–Jan Young, Executive Director, The Assisi Foundation of Memphis, Inc., Memphis, TN

DIAGNOSIS:
POVERTY

A new approach to
understanding and
treating an epidemic

Wilson, Marcella, PhD
Diagnosis: Poverty—A new approach to understanding and treating an epidemic
169 pp.
References: pp. 151–161

ISBN: 978-1-938248-76-4

aha! Process, Inc.
P.O. Box 727
Highlands, TX 77562-0727
(800) 424-9484 • (281) 426-5300
Fax: (281) 426-5600
Website: www.ahaprocess.com

Copy editing by Dan Shenk
Cover design by Amy Alick Perich

Names: Wilson, Marcella, author.
Title: Diagnosis: poverty : a new approach to understanding and treating an
            epidemic / by Marcella Wilson.
Description: Highlands, TX : aha! Process, Inc., [2017] | Includes bibliographical
            references.
Identifiers: ISBN: 978-1-938248-76-4 | LCCN: 2016956131
Subjects: LCSH: Poverty--United States. | Poverty--Government policy--United
          States. | Poor--United States. | Poor--Government policy--United States.
          | Poor--Services for--United States. | Social service--United States--
          Standards. | Poor--Medical care--United States--Standards. | Public welfare-
          -United States. | United States--Social conditions--21st century. | United
          States--Economic conditions--21st century.
Classification: LCC: HV95 .W55 2017 | DDC: 361.6/10973--dc23

Printed in the United States of America
10 9 8 7 6 5 4 3 2 1

DIAGNOSIS:
POVERTY

A new approach to
understanding and
treating an epidemic

By Marcella Wilson, PhD

Table of Contents

Prologue

In early 2016, as I left my position as CEO at Matrix Human Services and began my next evolution by writing this book, I took a few moments to reflect on what has been for me a remarkable, 10-year, life-changing journey.

I came to Matrix with three defined goals:

- To stabilize a 100-year-old charity
- To return to my social-work roots
- To do something meaningful before retiring

A five-year plan, retiring at age 53 and finally enjoying the benefits of being with a husband who not only could support me but wanted to. A grand, best-laid plan.

Ten years ago I never dreamed retirement would no longer be of interest because I would discover what has become my life's work. I never dreamed that playing a key role in a social movement and bringing voice to hope and change would consume my life. Ten years ago I had no idea that what I consider divine intervention would lead me to Matrix in Detroit, the poorest urban setting in the nation, for a profound and life-altering reason.

Many of the dreams of 10 years ago have been realized. Today Matrix is a thriving not for profit, recognized nationally and serving thousands of our nation's poorest. Today I have a new dream. This dream is of a country that attacks poverty as the epidemic it is, an epidemic eroding the fabric of the United States. My dream is of a nation that finally recognizes that poverty is not a flaw of character, a nation that realizes no one wants to be poor, without heat or access to fresh food or water or electricity.

This journey has taught me that no one wants to take the bus forever or see their children get sick over and over again because of deteriorated living conditions. No one wants to be afraid to walk to school or the store. Young men don't dream of going to prison or getting murdered before the age of 21. The crack-addicted baby, the hungry child, the unwanted teen, the homebound senior forced to choose between food and medications … All are surviving in a cruel and unequal society saturated with good intentions. No one wants to be poor.

I ask our nation, "What kind of America is ours when those most in need—our own children, families, veterans, and seniors—feel shame when asking for food, a place to sleep, or a helping hand?" We reinforce this shame with every means test, income assessment, long line, unanswered calls, and disproportionate educational funding. Treating the poor as second-class citizens is a glaring example of our well-established and largely accepted U.S. caste system, a system that sets all too many of life's trajectories from the moment of conception.

Poverty is not a character flaw. Poverty is a condition, even an epidemic, that can and must be accurately and compassionately diagnosed and treated.

Chapter 1

Secret Shopper

Purpose

The purpose of this book is to tell a story and to change—either by degrees or wholesale—the way we understand, think about, and respond to poverty. If you agree with the new paradigm presented in this book, the goal is a call to action, a call to respond. I am hoping that upon reading *Diagnosis: Poverty* you too agree that we must change the way our country responds to poverty—through our government, healthcare organizations, human services, faith-based entities, and educational programs.

I will be asking you to join in a revolution. Poverty in the United States of America is at epidemic proportions, affecting the health, education, and economic fabric of our nation today and possibly for generations to come.

We can all agree: Progressives and the spiritually grounded know it is morally right to care for and work with those less fortunate. The fiscally inclined also agree: Moving people off assistance is a high priority. This is a win-win. We can satisfy both sides of the fence with a realistic approach to attacking poverty. An approach that is more than just political rhetoric, prayer, or pie-in-the-sky fantasy. An approach that is real and tangible today.

I am an experienced and successful businesswoman. I have been a part of and led large corporations, each one growing under my leadership. Over a 30-year career I also have failed many times. Willingness to fail is a key ingredient of leadership—and, ironically, fear-induced paralysis is a root cause of failure. Thomas Edison, one of my heroes, once admitted that he failed 10,000 times before he successfully invented the electric light bulb.

Although apprehensive about what I might discover, I pretend to be a customer every time I start a new company or take over an existing company. It's one of my first orders of business. I call it being a secret shopper. I secretly "shop" at my own company and at my competitors' businesses … I do it regularly and on an ongoing basis.

I've learned the importance of continuous quality improvement (CQI). If you want to know what really goes on, look through the lens of the customer. Successful leadership requires a continuous loop of learning. Learn what is being done well and improve it; learn what customers want by simply asking them. Identify what needs improvement, then do it better than anyone else. This is CQI.

My secret-shopper approach to understanding and managing businesses has served me well, providing vital insight into what is most important in business. Customers drive profits. Without customers, there is no business, and my primary business, healthcare, is big business. Without satisfied customers, there is limited opportunity for growth and profits in any business. This was my world.

For 30 years I perfected my secret-shopper technique. I became an expert, pretending to be a patient seeking referrals, exceptions to care, and specialized services. Along the way I learned I can role-play anyone with any issue or problem imaginable.

Understanding customers began when I started my first business in high school, selling incense candles for a dollar to help cover my tuition. Each candle cost 10 cents to make, wax-scented with incense oil that covered the smell of pot. Hey, it was the '70s … Know your customers. I made lots of cash, a dollar at a time. I learned what customers wanted. That was business. From candlemaker to waitress to restaurant manager to healthcare, I learned the value of knowing both your customer and your competition.

In healthcare I knew what to ask for:

- "I need an out-of-network referral."
- "I need a medication outside of the formulary."
- "I need a specialist for an unusual diagnosis."

I tracked phone wait times, waiting-room wait times, response times for returned calls from the insurer and healthcare provider. I worked with the best teams using research, evaluation, and analytics to continually evolve products and delivery systems.

In healthcare knowing your customer also means knowing what conditions are costing the most money. While I was running a large, managed health plan for the chronically mentally ill, statistics indicated that many patients were being readmitted shortly after discharge from the hospital for exactly the same condition. Readmissions mean increased costs. Keeping patients out of the hospital is key to containing costs.

Many patients in Detroit were unable to afford and/or access transportation to their doctor appointments, leading to lapses in medications and re-hospitalizations. Even when patients got to their appointments, the chances of getting there on time were slim. Transportation services in the Detroit area were completely unreliable. The solution? We began providing taxi vouchers at the time of discharge, not a covered benefit. With this new benefit, patients had access to their medications. Paying for taxis decreased admissions to the hospital for chronically mentally ill patients. Our customers were more satisfied, costs decreased, profits increased, and every month for five years we experienced growing enrollment of new members.

A transportation voucher to a physician appointment was the right thing to do, and it improved the corporate bottom line. Win-win.

So after 25 years in healthcare, I was now leading Matrix Human Services in Detroit. It was time once again for secret shopper! I had a new character to portray and no experience in the role. This time I wasn't a patient with health insurance attempting to get care. I was instead going to be poor—a single mother in Detroit with a teen, tween, and Head Start baby. This was my fictitious persona. I didn't realize my secret-shopper experience, pretending to be poor, was about to change the trajectory of my life personally and professionally. My unscientific experiment became the catalyst not only for my personal transformation but also for a budding transformational movement in the United States.

A change that redefines America's understanding of what it is to be poor, who is poor, why they are poor, and what needs to be done about poverty will, I believe, significantly transform our nation's response to poverty, treating it as the condition it is, not as a character flaw. No one wants to be poor. The sheer volume of Americans living in poverty from the moment of their birth would seem evidence enough. Allow me to restate: Poverty is not a character flaw.

- In 2016 about 70 million Americans were enrolled in Medicaid.[1]

- How many people is 70 million? By comparison, the population of Canada is 35 million.

- Also by comparison, 7.6 million people in the U.S. have cancer.

- 70 million people on Medicaid, and 46.7 million—14.8% of all Americans—lived below the poverty line in America in 2014.[2]

- It isn't overstating the case to say that poverty has reached epidemic proportions in the United States of America, one of the richest nations in the world.

That secret shopper in the spring of 2006, pretending to be a poor single woman with three children in Detroit, changed everything. Now I see the world, my life's work, and the reason for this book: to change how this country understands and responds to the condition of poverty.

This is that story

I mentioned Matrix, but a bit more backstory is needed.

My 40s were not easy. Although my career in the healthcare field was going great guns, my marriage was in crisis. With family as my priority, I left an executive position in a national managed healthcare company for a local managed healthcare position. No more travel around the country, less stress, more time with family. A stable, challenging, well-paying local job. My mother couldn't have been happier. Even with the new job and lots of counseling, however, my husband and I divorced after 20 years of marriage.

At this point I learned a powerful life lesson, found (of all places) on the wrapper of a Dove chocolate bar that remains on my refrigerator to this day: "Love many, trust few, always paddle your own canoe."

Although my life changed dramatically, the ability to support myself and my two children, the ability to keep us in our home (with the pool) and their private schools was never lost on me. Watching so many of my friends and colleagues lose so much in divorce, I knew I was blessed. My education was my life preserver, and I was able to support myself and my children.

Life continued as a single mother, raising my children, when a new and exciting opportunity presented itself: a CEO position at a local managed-care startup based in Detroit, with an annual budget of $150 million. I was up for the challenge. My dream job began, but it was quickly turning into a nightmare. This startup was like no other. Little did I know that these times were about to be among the darkest days in Detroit's history. A young, dynamic Mayor Kwame Kilpatrick was nonetheless wreaking havoc on the city. His escapades and those of his complicit father, Bernard, appointed by his son as chair of the Community Mental Health Board in Detroit, would later become public fodder and national news. Much evidence points to the fact that their corruption was blatant.

Given the fact that I look awful in orange and refused to play the game, getting anything done in the City of Detroit, where the majority of the startup's enrollees lived, became next to impossible. The pay-to-play mentality was thriving. Although our organization was very well-funded, my ability to get services delivered to those most in need was a source of nearly constant angst. As my frustration mounted, so did my desire to return to my original, chosen profession of social work. After just five years, I left the managed-care startup.

My search for a new job began. Armed with my PhD, years of experience and, most importantly, a master's in social work, I was ready to lead a charity. I wanted to get back to my roots and do something meaningful before I retired. Perhaps a delusional notion, but that was my thought process.

Enter Matrix

Enter Matrix Human Services. Then celebrating its hundredth anniversary, Matrix, a Detroit-based not for profit, needed a CEO. The charity, which was providing a variety of services to about 10,000 low-income individuals and families annually in greater Detroit, was in dire straits financially and facing bankruptcy. Foolishly and naively, I believed that not for profits are immune to political tampering and corruption … It's a charity, after all. I convinced the Matrix board's search committee to hire me. And so it began.

Although Matrix was mired in financial issues, what I discovered there was a new world. Matrix 2006 was virtually unknown in the community, with an annual posted budget (no accurate records to be found) of $17 million, a plethora of underfunded programs, clients of all ages in great need, a stock of dilapidated buildings, a disengaged board, a hostile union, and vendors in hot pursuit.

I also found some of the most dedicated, well-meaning, and caring employees I had ever encountered. Although Matrix was a fiscal disaster, it was evident immediately that much of the work being done was nothing short of profound.

During my first week of employment, like a teenage girl with a first crush, I fell fast and hard. It was during this first week that my completely unscientific, life-changing experiment took place.

In my lovely office in mid-town Detroit, with a full stomach and an unending supply of hot black coffee (thank you, Miss Shirley), I pretended to be poor—on the phone. With my new identity as a single mother with three children, a phone with unlimited minutes, the ability to read, write, and speak English, along with a phone book and the Yellow Pages, I began my attempt to access services for myself and my pretend family.

So, what do I know about being poor? Next to nothing. I was raised by white immigrant parents in a middle-class family in the suburbs. I never knew hunger—or went without heat or water. Other than a school bus, tour bus, or private bus for an event, I had never taken a bus anywhere. Our schools were rated among the best in the nation, our neighborhoods were safe and, as a child of an autoworker protected by the union, my father earned a living wage and had some of the best healthcare in the nation. I heard the stories of the early tough times when my parents and my very young siblings arrived in America from Malta. I was born later. Their dream for me was college.

Posing as poor in my first days at Matrix, I was totally and completely out of my element. I spent two days on the phone attempting to secure services for myself and my pretend family. The response (or lack thereof) was shocking. I made dozens of calls to government offices, healthcare organizations, Head Start, workforce development, shelters, and social service agencies—all with my sincere desire to turn my pretend life around. In just two days the reality became crystal-clear. I got no direction, no support. I soon lost hope that I would get help. One hoop after another and not a single call returned.

I even called several of the 40 Matrix offices around the city. As a secret shopper, I was unable to access services even at the organization I was now leading! I received the same story over and over again …

when the phone was actually answered: I didn't qualify, I didn't live in the right ZIP Code, I had to be referred by the courts, and if I did actually get through, there were no program openings and no other options offered. To this day all those other calls remain unreturned.

Even though my experience of pretending to be poor was superficial at best, I knew something was very wrong. My teenage crush on Matrix, love for this new job and the people we were serving, also was met with profound heartache, a heartache borne from witnessing, day after day, the pain and suffering that poverty brings to so many. Coming to work to witness hunger from our youngest client of age 3 to our oldest of 103—and knowing I now had the responsibility to address it—felt overwhelming.

Michelle

The first Matrix client I met in person was Michelle.

Her mother died when she was just a little girl. Michelle was born into poverty in Detroit. Her family was always poor. She was abused physically, mentally, and sexually throughout her life. As a teen she ran away from home, lived on the streets and continued to go to school. Her once promising basketball career vanished; in its place a relationship with drugs took control. She was victimized, abandoned, and forgotten.

Now, fresh out of substance-abuse treatment, her dream was to live clean and take care of her two children. Michelle's story affected me deeply and helped me understand, for the first time, on an intensely personal level the struggles and realities of poverty. That first week, in my office, we cried together.

Michelle was, and continues to be, an inspiration to me and so many others. To this day she fuels my determination. This woman wanted so desperately to have a new life. It became very clear to me, however, that she had no idea how to accomplish that goal—and no one in her life outside of Matrix to support or teach her. Michelle's words explained it all: "In poverty people want to get better; they just don't know how."

Hearing Michelle's story, seeing what I was seeing, feeling helpless in an organization with limited resources, I was determined to do something to help her and the thousands of other clients we were serving. This is how my life-changing journey began.

Chapter 2

Are You Kidding Me?

From the frying pan into the fire

The diversity of our Matrix customer base was rich ... the largest Head Start in the city of Detroit, operating in three languages: English, Spanish, and Arabic; senior-service programs, including homebound seniors; juvenile justice; after-school programs; runaway shelter for teens; residential foster care; and a small but significant shelter for men with HIV/AIDS. Who knew running a not for profit was going to be the toughest management gig of my career. I had gone from the frying pan into the fire.

Despite my excitement about my new job, I quickly discovered that a not-for-profit human-service agency can be the most counterproductive business environment imaginable, operating in a culture that promotes dependency, inefficiencies and, most troubling, a complete lack of quality-improvement processes for its customers. Not for profits have low margins (if any), constant scrutiny, declining reimbursements, fierce competition, and rigid funding mechanisms in an industry where demand exceeding supply is *not* a good thing.

Not-for-profit management in human services can be downright daunting. Where else are you required to include begging in your skill set? I know, we don't call it begging. The politically correct descriptions are "development" and "fundraising." I say, "A rose is a rose is a rose." Truth be told, there is a thriving, multi-million-dollar industry dedicated and designed to support the education and accreditation of fund-raising professionals. The begging industry has a complete infrastructure supporting the development of begging skills and begging methodology. It's an industry designed to continually improve the way we ask people and corporations for their money to support the not-for-profit mission.

What a concept: I will scratch your back, you get to feel good, I get money, and you get a tax deduction. I quickly learned the drill. These precious, donated funds are essential to run the not-for-profit industry. Solicited donations known as unrestricted funds are essential to fix holes in roofs, mow the lawns, pay the heating bill, meet budget shortfalls, buy blankets ... the list goes on and on. But such essentials are excluded by most funders from most awards.

For example, the funder awards $1,000 for care management for runaway teens, but it doesn't allow the money to be spent on kids' haircuts or driver's education. The rules, regulations, and restrictions are endless and speak to society's need to ensure that every dollar is managed and accounted for—and that no one receives services unless those services "fit the description," regardless of program or client need.

Knowing charity begins at home, I began to hone my begging skills, first with my mother. At age 82 my immigrant mother was sharp as a tack. Throughout my life I watched both my parents donate within their means, including the tithing expected in our traditional Roman Catholic household. Mother Teresa became her favorite cause and donating outside of the Catholic world was not readily embraced. I pitched Matrix, but Mom wanted to see the financials and program descriptions. I dutifully provided the "new" marketing materials designed specifically to open strangers' wallets.

A personal family connection

In short order, my dear mother began shrieking with delight. Matrix began as the League of Catholic Women and provided support to my parents and siblings when they immigrated to the United States in 1950. (Let's be clear; I was not yet born.) My mother shared her story of the organization's support, referred by their church, as they adjusted to a new country, new customs, and economic challenges.

Mom recalled her embarrassment when my siblings came home from after-school programming with new "gym shoes." The kids were excited; my mother was aghast. Her interpretation? The church sent home these shoes because the ones her children were wearing were not acceptable. Her reaction was one of shame and confusion. A culture clash of a different era. Today sneakers are a part of U.S. culture, but in the '50s and '60s gym shoes were required footwear for school gymnasiums. My mother had no idea what a gymnasium even was. The shoes were sent home for after-school gym.

Just like today in immigrant families, my older siblings served as the cultural teachers in a new world. Just like today, the shame of poverty, the embarrassment of being judged, and the character-flaw mentality were consistent and powerful forces.

I was astounded to learn of my family's connection more than a half-century earlier with the charity I now led. I knew of my family's struggles as new immigrants in Detroit; I had heard stories about hard times, not enough money, grueling winters, and my parents doing without boots and coats in the cold northern weather. Just like Julie Andrews in "The Sound of Music," my mother made clothes from curtains! We love these family stories of the hard times, overcoming struggles, and realizing the American dream. But not until that day, when I asked for a donation for the poor, did I realize why their stories never included their experience with a charity. Giving to charity is glorified; the government's tax system even rewards it. Fundraising, volunteering, or working for a charity is noble. But *needing* charity tends to be a closely guarded secret.

I got the check for Matrix from my mother. I was on a roll. The scope of my begging soon expanded to the world of foundations and government entities. It sounded so good. Foundations and government contracts designed specifically to give away money and support worthy causes … one of which I was now leading.

Easy, breezy, beautiful, right? Not so fast. Name one other industry where you are given funding with these types of caveats … "We will give you half the money you need for this specific cause and this specific purpose, but you must fund-raise (beg) for the rest, and if you don't raise the rest of the money, we will take our portion back." Are you kidding me? Imagine this: "We will give you half the money you need to build our plane, fight our war, build our building, but you must come up with the rest." Who does business like this?

The real kicker: Not for profits engage in fierce competition to secure financial backing, then thank funders profusely even for limited, insufficient funding. Regardless of the rules, regulations, caveats, and limitations, I learned quite quickly that not-for-profit competition is fierce. Don't let the soft veneers and compelling stories fool you.

The competition factor

The 25 largest not for profits in southeast Michigan had a combined $7 billion in 2012 gross receipts.[3] In Detroit the number and diversity of charities are plentiful, exceeded only by the demand for their services. Leaders in the not for profits, much like our customers, are always looking for ways to make things happen and get some cash in the door. It is, after all, business. Just like a business, dollars drive the products offered.

So when a foundation or funder puts out a precious bid, not for profits from across the community submit their proposals, often with little regard for their not-for-profit brothers and sisters currently offering the same service as their core business, their lifeblood. This mentality of eat or be eaten is often palpable, breeding mistrust and undermining collaboration and integration across the "silos" of care (each entity working on its own, essentially oblivious to what others in the helping professions are doing). If I support your organization and your services, your ability to compete against me for donations, contracts, and media attention is enhanced.

The common behavior of not for profits is like the swarm mentality in peewee sports. Little kids, just learning the sport, all run toward the ball. That's what they do. It doesn't matter if it's a basketball, soccer ball, baseball, or football ... no team strategy. No teamwork. They swarm to the ball. If there is funding, we all go after it! Survival of the fittest. Follow the money.

I eventually learned, to my dismay, that the not-for-profit competition is no-holds-barred, with little attention paid to gaps, delivery-system analysis, and development of consistent and meaningful performance measures across multiple sectors.

I jumped in, all in, to the swarm mentality of the community-based not for profit. Fund it, and they will come.

Chapter 3

Who Knew?

'Do you see what I see?'

As my not-for-profit education continued, my most pressing need was money to keep the doors open and service for the thousands of clients coming into our programs, all in need—many in desperate need.

In those first weeks I toured all of the many Matrix facilities.

Welcome to the Mt. Zion church, located in the Osborn neighborhood in Detroit. This building was donated to Matrix years ago for $1, then was abandoned by the Lutheran congregation that, like so many others, moved to the suburbs. Once boasting a parishioner enrollment of thousands, the building now sat nearly empty, a cold behemoth with a large cross at its doors and 60,000 square feet of frigid, dark space.

Arriving at the old church on Gratiot Avenue was like entering a war zone. I had never seen anything like it in my life in the United States of America. Burnt-out buildings, trash everywhere, boarded-up buildings. The only signs of life were found driving past the payday-lender outlets, beauty salons, and liquor stores.

I arrived to see this massive Matrix building surrounded by litter-strewn alleys and broken streets, broken windows, a broken neighborhood. I realized our Head Start children, housed in the basement of this building, walked by all this every day on the way to their classrooms. With the possibility of flying bullets, I knew that going outside for recess was not an option for these children. Their reality, now under my watch, was simply heartbreaking. This once pristine place of worship was now filthy, with shattered windows, junk stacked high, and evidence of rodents and roaches. In the basement, where I visited the small Head Start program, the smell of sewage made me gasp. These beautiful children, so full of life, seemed unconcerned. Having no idea who I was, they rushed to hug me, all at once. Swarming isn't just for sports! Their welcome to me as a guest touched my heart. The teachers, working in this environment, knew who I was—and they hoped and pleaded that I would be able to do something. There wasn't anger, just pleading. I promised I would try.

My tour continued. On the first floor, in a back hall near a ladies room, I found her. A homeless woman. I was quickly advised by Center Director Scott that Mary arrives in the morning, stays all day, leaves when the building closed. No one knew where she went. Mary was severely overweight, older in years, clearly had all her belongings with her and appeared to be wearing most of them. Everyday staff offered her whatever food was available. Her presence was obvious, yet oblivious. The Matrix world went on around her as if having a homeless woman living in your lobby, using your facilities, were a normal occurrence.

I stopped to speak with Mary, and it was instantly clear that our Mary was delusional. Staff had no idea who she was or where she was from. As I spoke with Mary and with staff, it took all my strength. The Matrix staff persons were anxious to see my reaction to the situation. Irritation? Intolerance? Compassion? I asked, "Do you see what I see?"

A crying shame

CEOs are not supposed to weep at work. That day and in the succeeding days I kept telling myself this in hopes it would actually take hold; it seldom did. Not crying at work became my new professional challenge.

Over the next few weeks taking care of Mary became a Matrix priority. As a senior citizen with chronic mental illness, Mary was eligible for a plethora of services. Actualizing those services, however, was a whole 'nother story. Mary proved, without a shadow of doubt, that a healthcare card and eligibility to services was not access, especially for those most in need. For our team, not specifically funded to support someone like Mary, holding several independent, disconnected systems accountable was formidable. Working together, we defined the services Mary was eligible for and what organizations were responsible for caring for her, then together we demanded action on her behalf.

Our work as her advocates took us straight to the doors of CEOs of other organizations being paid to care for her. Mary was our client, purely by adoption, and we were insisting on service. Although we did eventually get some care, housing, and medical support for Mary, we now understood why Mary had no hope. The system designed and paid for to take care of Mary was sadly ineffective for anyone without the ability and resources to navigate the complex apparatus of care.

Mary's case made it crystal-clear. By and large, the system wasn't working for the poor. The institutions paid to care for Mary were not being held responsible by the people they were caring for. Their responsibility was primarily to funders and the bottom line. I now knew that most poor people (even pretend ones with a PhD and the ability to read) aren't very well-equipped to navigate the complex delivery systems of healthcare, human services, and government and education programs. Sick people, especially children, are at even higher risk.

As someone who had been sheltered from the hardships of poverty all my life, I have yet to learn how to cope with it. Recalling these stories brings emotion right back to the surface. I would note that through the efforts of a dedicated staff and the response we received from other providers, Mary was finally taken care of, yet so many people continue to experience the same kinds of hardships every day.

I had seen all the heart-wrenching commercials, photos of hungry children living in unsanitary conditions, but this was different, and it affected me more than anything in my professional life. As I toured Matrix programs and surrounding neighborhoods, what I saw was shocking, so sad, and simply unacceptable. Thousands of clients, all in various states of need, hunger, sickness, hopelessness. And it was all happening just 35 minutes from my home in beautiful West Bloomfield where residents live in upscale comfort.

As I toured Matrix programs, I was practically speechless. I saw government-funded housing programs with no running water, our clients living in squalor, and mothers afraid to complain because there were no other options. Homeless teens, many of them abused and never reported missing, entering our shelter programs and residential units with their belongings in a couple of garbage bags, along with children of all ages hoarding food for fear of hunger. Everywhere I looked I saw people (including Matrix employees) in need, many of them also living at or near poverty levels, attempting to help within the guidelines of funding and budget. The need tremendous, the response sincere, our impact … who knows?

Indeed, everywhere I looked I saw poor people, and no one seemed to be getting better. I asked what would become for me a critical question, "How do you treat poverty?"

My research began. I needed to first understand the scope and enormity of the problem. Statistics tell at least part of the alarming story. I learned that 56,900 children, birth to 5, were living in Detroit, and 57% of them were in poverty, the highest of any urban setting in the nation.[4] I also learned that 67% of Detroit children lived in neighborhoods with concentrated poverty.[5] And I learned that Detroit had the highest infant and maternal death rates in the country; infant mortality was double the national average.[6]

Here are other sobering stats about Detroit:

- Forty percent of expectant mothers do not receive pre-natal care.[7]

- More than 200,000 residents, or 47% of the adult population, are "functionally illiterate," according to the Detroit Workforce Fund Report.[8]

- Seniors, ages 50–59, are dying at a rate 122% higher than their counterparts elsewhere in Michigan.[9]

The state of poverty in Detroit was shocking and remains so. My research continued, and Detroit was not alone.

In Michigan 16.2% of the population, or 1,688,000 people, were living in poverty—enough to fill Comerica Park, home of the Detroit Tigers, 40 times.[10]

In Michigan nearly one of every four children (492,000 children statewide) lived in poverty, with child poverty rates increasing from 18% to 22.6% between 2007 and 2014.[11]

I learned that 69% of homeless families were headed by women, and the average age of a homeless child in Michigan was 7.[12]

Most startling, 40% of households across Michigan struggled to pay for the basic necessities of housing, childcare, food, healthcare, and transportation.[13]

As Detroit goes, so goes Michigan. And so goes the country?

Allow me to present further statistics, especially as they relate to the United States as a whole—and how this country compares to other developed countries around the world.

- In the U.S., "the land of opportunity," 48.8 million, or 16% of the population, is living in poverty.[14]

- In this nation a child is born into poverty every 33 seconds—22% of children in the U.S.[15]

- The U.S. ranks second highest in child poverty among the world's richest 35 countries, surpassed only by Romania.[16]

- How big is the problem? The number of people living in poverty in the U.S. increased by 49% between 1996 and 2011, while the population grew by only 13%.[17]

- In this country babies die within their first week of life twice as often as infants in Norway, Portugal, and the Czech Republic.[18]

- In the United States almost half of children born to low-income parents become low-income adults.[19]

- Among developed countries where data are available, the U.S. has the highest infant mortality rate, highest teenage birthrate, and highest incarceration rate (we house 22% of the world's prisoners).[20]

- In the U.S. nearly 45% of all children (more than 32 million) live in low-income families.[21]

- Almost three-quarters of single-mother families are low-income.[22]

- Illustrating glaring issues of racial inequity, about 65% of African American, Native American, and Hispanic children live in low-income families compared with 32% of Caucasian and Asian American children.[23]

- Boys growing up in poverty are more likely to be arrested as adults, and their female peers are more likely to give birth outside of marriage.[24]

- Children under 18 represent 23% of the population, but they comprise 32% of all people in poverty.[25]

- In a Gallup survey, a staggering one in six Americans reported they couldn't afford food at times within the past year.[26]

The mind-blower

Then came the mind-blower. Even low levels of food insecurity directly affect the development of children's brains, specifically white matter, gray matter, and the hippocampus.[27]

I was stunned. Although well-substantiated in the research, this was the first time I read this and understood its true implications. As CEO at Matrix I was now responsible for 1,300 children, 3 to 5 years of age, five days a week, nine months a year. I was seeing these beautiful children and realizing that, statistically, children growing up in poverty complete less schooling, have less work, and earn less money as adults—and are more likely to receive public assistance and have poor health.[28]

Taken together, the scope of the problem, the racial inequities, the realization that lack of nutritious food directly affects brain development and future generations hit me as profoundly tragic.

To a significant degree, the futures of these 1,300 children were now in our hands, and our responsibility was no longer just running a Head Start. The Matrix clientele also included homeless men with HIV/AIDS, runaways, teens who were in foster care or homeless, and a fragile elderly population. As I more clearly understood the reality of their lives, their struggles, and the lost opportunities perpetrated in many cases by "the system," my personal and professional commitment to get beyond business as usual became consuming.

Chapter 4

Show Me the Money

How can this be?

Poverty's sheer numbers, much less impact, in the United States are almost beyond comprehension. How can this be? In the greatest country in the world, how can this happen?

As part of my initial efforts at Matrix, I was told by many: "It's a funding problem!" The system, improperly funded, can't respond to the never-ending stream of clients. OK, that made sense. I knew Matrix could barely make ends meet, and I saw no indication that the people we were serving were "living the life." In fact, it was quite the opposite.

I was called to the offices of City of Detroit Head Start, the funder for Head Start in Detroit.

I get to the building, nowhere to park, the lot behind is locked, with employee cars safely tucked away. Customers, the poor, are on their own. No attendant in sight. The street is filled with abandoned and burnt-out houses; trash is everywhere, either scattered or in large piles on lots. There's no one in the streets. A dog walks slowly in the opposite direction. I park down the street at the first available space. I walk quickly.

Finally I'm in the building. It's dark, bulbs burnt out. It's also dirty, like the walls and floors haven't been washed in years. Two security guards sit causally talking; one nods to direct me to sign in. "Eighth floor," he says and points to the elevator. Like the building and surroundings, the elevator is old. It looks old, smells old.

Ah, the eighth floor, the penthouse. I arrive, and the surroundings remain decrepit. I am led to a conference room so jammed with office furniture you can barely get through the aisles. A small place at the front of the room provides the perch for the director to give her assembled minions, Head Start providers, their marching orders.

We're sitting in storage space with over a dozen human-services executives squashed into the room, with no water and no apology. The heat is oppressive. It's winter in Detroit and bitterly cold outside, but inside this government building it's downright tropical. What a waste—and what a message to those seeking services.

The meeting finally ends, and I'm asked to stay to meet with the director. As others are ushered to the elevators, I am led to another door marked "Administration." The door opens, and the oppressive waiting room becomes the Department of Human Services oasis. There are air conditioners blowing cool air; fresh paint, lighting, and beautiful cherrywood furniture grace the inner sanctum. We have our meeting.

I return to the first floor. The guards remain in the same positions. I look at the one leaning on the desk. "Sir, please see me out," I say. "I think your customers would be better served if you were outside." He shakes his head and grudgingly walks me out. I was simply asking for what we as customers need and expect—an example of why we cannot just stand by and watch if we truly want change. I believe that assertive advocacy is key to directly addressing social injustice in all its forms.

Behavior unchallenged is behavior unchanged

My experience dealing with the system to help the poor in Detroit was a reflection of the reality of services in Detroit. The dysfunction, however, is more complex and widespread in this country than the time-limited scandal in Detroit. (Not too long after that meeting the pricey furniture would play a part in one of many news stories that exposed the Kilpatrick administration's abuse of those they were entrusted to protect. According to the allegations, funds allocated for appliances for Detroit's poorest residents were used instead to buy fancy furniture for executives. The Head Start director left. A few years later so did Kilpatrick, but he went to prison, followed soon by his father.)

The general consensus in Detroit—and with many people I spoke to—was that there wasn't enough money to care for the millions living in poverty in this country.

My research continued. Much to my surprise, I discovered that the United States of America has the most extensive and expensive delivery system in world history to help the poor.[29]

Treating Poverty in the U.S.

'Siloed' Spending and Service

The current disconnected service delivery system in the United States

$ 1,660,451,000,000

Human Services	Education	Healthcare	Government
◆ 1.4 million not for profits	◆ 99,000 public schools	◆ 5,723 hospitals	◆ DHS
◆ 650,000 social workers	◆ 3.7 million elementary and secondary teachers	◆ 209,000 PCPs	◆ Community mental health
	◆ 262,300 school counselors	◆ Medicaid health plans	◆ Housing
		◆ Medicare health plans	◆ Medicaid/Medicare
			◆ Veterans
			◆ Juvenile justice
			◆ Prisoner reentry

Source: http://www.whitehouse.gov/sites/default/files/omb/budget/fy2013/assets/hist.pdf

© 2016 Transition To Success®

According to a 2011 edition of *Stanford Social Innovation Review,*

government units at all levels in the U.S. devote more than 1 trillion, 165 billion dollars annually to poverty issues. This does not include the funding generated from individual and corporate donations, foundations, and the powerful impact of the faith-based community.

In the U.S. 1.4 million not for profits are devising independent solutions to major social problems, and 86,000 charitable foundations are funding "siloed" solutions.[30] The Bridgespan Group adds:

By their very nature, individual, not-for-profit services are fragmented and dispersed, with each organization typically serving a limited population with a specific intervention. Funders then measure success at the organizational level, not the broader community.[31]

These statistics don't include the costs related to the criminal-justice system. In the United States 2.3 million people (about 90% male) are incarcerated at a cost of $80 billion annually.[32]

"Unnatural Causes: In Sickness and in Health" (2008) states:

> The stats about the poor also don't include the fact that in the U.S. we spend $2 trillion per year on medical care (nearly half of all dollars spent in the world), yet we live shorter, often sicker, lives than residents of almost every industrialized nation.[33]

There is, of course, a strong link between poverty and health. See the next chapter—and especially Chapter 6—for more about that.

According to the National Center for Charitable Statistics (NCCS), more than 1.5 million not-for-profit organizations are registered in the United States. This includes public charities, private foundations, and other types of not-for-profit organizations.[34]

The trillion-dollar industry of "caring for the poor" is further supplemented by the predatory-lending industry that permeates the economics of poverty. Payday lending, throwaway phones, check-cashing outlets, and pawn shops are all thriving industries, compounded by exorbitant interest rates, penalties, and policies that take advantage of and penalize the poor. In this country 48 million "customers" live in poverty.[35]

The U.S. devotes more resources than many other nations to pensions, healthcare, family support, food, unemployment checks, housing assistance, and similar benefits—all meant to help people in hard times. Compared with most advanced countries, the U.S. gets far less cost benefit in terms of health outcomes and equality.[36]

So why is it, in this trillion-dollar industry of helping the poor, that this country's treatment of the poor, our customers, is so abysmal?

Chapter 5

The Character-Flaw Mentality

'Badatude'

Treating the poor poorly has deep roots in our American history. From our beginnings as a nation, there has been a "badatude" (bad attitude) toward the poor, differentiation between the deserving and undeserving poor, and stigma attached to being poor.

In the United States, during the first three decades of the 20th century, The Charity Organization Societies sought to make a distinction between "the deserving poor ... and the lazybones who would not work."[37] In contrast, during the same time period, the settlement house movement tried to avoid stereotyping the poor, offering educational and cultural supports.

Rooted in U.S. history, classism, negative attitudes, and discrimination toward others—based on their low economic status—have been pervasive, fostering antagonism and even contempt for the poor. The many negative messages about the poor being deficient and inferior drive the devaluation of people living in poverty.[38] Further, research clearly shows, "Social class is the most important determinant of health, above any other risk factor."[39]

The character-flaw mentality came home to roost at Matrix. It was hard times in Detroit. Massive unemployment, a city in bankruptcy, recession, and the collapse of the auto industry in, of all places, the Motor City. I was chagrined that many of our employees also could qualify as our clients. Imagine my sadness when it was reported to me by a program executive that one of our employees was found Dumpster diving at one of our sites. I was dismayed when asked if I wanted to follow up with disciplinary action. After all, what kind of example was this woman setting?

Such an attitude remained widespread, even at the highest level in our own organization. Imagine the embarrassment for this young woman: being "caught in the act." Many low-income individuals perceive welfare participation as stigmatizing.[40] Yet the shame was ours because one of our own could not ask for help.

Sometimes 'Work hard and prosper' doesn't work

The character-flaw mentality—namely, that select individuals and groups are in poverty due to their own misdeeds and sinful habits and that their situation is somehow a punishment requiring penance, and recovery is their own responsibility—is well-established in our country's history and current national psyche. "Work hard and prosper" is often a fantasy not based in reality for millions of Americans. Tolerance, supposedly a cornerstone value in the U.S., is often in short supply.

In the December 13, 2015, edition of the *Baltimore Sun,* a front-page article titled "The Housing Trap" details a successful housing relocation project: "That relocation program—one of the nation's largest—has been discreetly rolled out to avoid the political and community opposition that routinely arises to defeat proposals for building subsidized housing in Baltimore's suburbs," writes reporter Doug Donovan.

"'We did it very much under the radar,'" said Amy Wilkinson, Fair Housing director for the Housing Authority of Baltimore City, of the home purchases. "'We met very early on with county executives …

Their request was to make sure [the homes] are really scattered and make sure we do it quietly.'"[41]

Imagine being one of the mothers in the relocated homes or, even worse, one of those children. Knowing you had to be discreet in your own neighborhood and school, knowing that "if they know the truth I could be humiliated, exposed or even lose my new life," continues Donovan. Although sensitive to the character-flaw mentality, program administrators had to find a way to make a good program work. The realistic strategy had to directly address the issues of intolerance and the character-flaw mentality of government and community. This approach is far simpler than dealing with the real problem: addressing the psychological impact on these mothers and children, knowing they have to keep who they are a secret in order to be accepted and take part in a life-changing opportunity.

In the suburbs of Baltimore, the fears of increased crime did not materialize, and none of the participants in the mobility program lost their housing subsidies due to criminal activity.

Reporter Donovan also cites a recent Harvard University study released in 2015 that indicates the Baltimore children, especially boys, have lower odds of escaping poverty than in any other city in the nation. Life's trajectory should not be determined by your ZIP Code.

Children tend to be the most frequent victims of the poverty cycle, blamed and shamed for circumstances beyond their control, and traumatized by a culture that all too often would rather focus on character flaws than the failure of a nation and its people to appropriately and effectively care for the most vulnerable among us.

Being born poor is not a character flaw, but for many it is a life sentence. There's chronic stress when dealing with crime, fear, racism, and discrimination—all the while trying to meet basic needs for oneself and one's children. Such traumatic circumstances can undermine hope.

'Learned helplessness'

In her book *A Framework for Understanding Poverty,* Ruby K. Payne explains one aspect of generational poverty, learned helplessness, which is passed from parents to children, over generations.[44] In addition to her well-known work with hidden rules and the importance of resources, Dr. Payne emphasizes the resiliency and problem-solving skills of people in poverty.

But part of the poverty picture for some—particularly those in generational poverty—is learned helplessness: a mental state in which an organism forced to bear aversive stimuli or stimuli that are painful or otherwise unpleasant, becomes unable or unwilling to avoid subsequent encounters with those stimuli, even if they're escapable.[45]

A dispiriting aspect of learned helplessness is ceasing to try as a result of consistently not being rewarded in life, and it is thought to be a cause of depression. Learned helplessness is characterized by decreased motivation, failure to learn, and such negative emotions as sadness, anxiety, and frustration. Learned helplessness has been recognized in both adults and children.

When animals, including humans, are repeatedly subjected to inescapable aversive stimuli, eventually the animal will stop trying to avoid the stimulus and behave as if it is completely powerless to change the situation. This is what happens with alarming frequency to those living in poverty.

My father tells the story of his hardships coming to the United States as a Maltese immigrant. My parents were poor, uneducated, and not conversant in English. They worked hard; my father held two jobs most of his life. They saved their money, bought a home in the suburbs, and raised four children. They are the American Dream immigrant story. They are white.

My parents came to this country, specifically Detroit, for that American Dream. My father landed his first job at Ford Motor Company in what he called "the pits." His job was to shovel coal into a huge furnace—the absolute worst job at the Ford River Rouge plant. He would come home burnt and exhausted. But he never missed a day. At work my father became friends with Al, his first friend of color. They had the same job, though I'm not sure if the pay was equal. As my father climbed on the seniority list he said to Al, "You're next to get out to the line [a better job on the assembly line], then I'm next."

Al schooled my father: "I will never get to the line; those jobs are not for Negroes." My father quickly learned that the good jobs, better wages, better schools, ability to buy a home, and the American Dream were intended for those with white skin who worked hard, not everyone who worked hard. A tragic American reality, often overlooked, especially by those who did make it. Finally, a clear and powerful rebuttal to the question: "I did it; why can't they?"

Racism—which often translates to lack of access to nutritious food, living-wage jobs, adequate housing, healthcare, clean air, clean water, decent schools, safe neighborhoods—is aversive and for too many, inescapable. This trap changes the trajectory of lives, communities, and nations for generations to come.

In 15th-century England—as the number of those living in poverty increased due to plagues, wars, and economic downturns—vagrancy laws were created, punishing beggars and vagrants with public whippings, exile, forced labor, slavery, even execution. Historically the response was based upon getting rid of the poor, not helping the poor.

Many British colonists coming to America brought these attitudes with them.[47] Boston established the first "poorhouse" in 1664. Other cities, including Philadelphia, New York, and Baltimore, followed suit. These poorhouses were never intended to care for the poor; rather they were "the best means of frightening the able bodied into going to work and discouraging people from applying for aid."[48]

Our system was designed to minimize and embarrass as a form of motivation. Shame them to change. Just like a mother who hangs her son's sheets out the window to change his bedwetting ways, this country's systems, policies, and pervasive attitudes have been to change behavior through fear, embarrassment, and shame.

Shame does not change behavior for bedwetters, for alcoholics and drug addicts, or for non-compliant diabetics. No one wants to wet the bed, be addicted, or lose a limb due to diabetes. And no one wants to be poor. All of these conditions require a scientific understanding of the problem in a system that continually redesigns and improves treatment based on research and data. This is the only effective way to change behavior for both the patient and the systems entrusted to care for them.

First a secret shopper, then a witness

My antennae became attuned to the character-flaw mentality—first as a disrespected and ignored secret shopper, then as a witness. It seems the general consensus among many in this nation is that the poor are lazy, the poor want everything for nothing, the poor take advantage of our generosity, the poor are the victims of their own making, and it is acceptable to provide the poor with terrible service in poorly maintained buildings, with little accountability in a culture where the customers sometimes even fear retribution. In U.S. society it seems the most important thing is to ensure that only the "worthy" poor reap the benefits of our generosity.

Our system to help the poor is based on eligibility and compliance policies and procedures with dehumanizing labels for customers created by those same organizations designed and funded to help them. This culture of poverty—driven by economics and unequal systems of health, housing, education, and employment—has created a class of people falsely perceived as lacking strengths and abilities simply because they are poor. There's a not-so-subtle, ongoing message here, from birth to death, that people in poverty are the problem and require fixing.

In a qualitative study of 19 low-income women published in "Cultural Diversity and Ethnic Minority Psychology," Erin Godfrey and psychologist Sharon Wolf found that almost all the participants attributed poverty to character flaws, lack of hard work, and other individual factors. Fewer than half cited structural explanations, and when they did it was almost always in tandem with individual explanations. "People were really relying on these myths about society—that you can get ahead if you just try hard enough," says Godfrey.[49]

In one of my unscientific surveys, I discovered that a proposed policy of discontinuing food benefits for mothers who test positive for drugs is a common position, not just within my social circle but for many of our own clients and many of my colleagues. Even many non-drug-addicted poor people supported the discontinuation of benefits to addicted moms and their families. In other words, to promote compliance and reduce drug addiction, let's stop feeding addicts and their children.

Imagine a new single mother, living with limited resources: limited phone minutes, limited access to food and transportation, and little money. Given her very limited resources, what are the chances that she will use precious phone minutes to schedule her or her baby's follow-up appointments, most likely on two different days at two different locations? Just the wait time to schedule appointments eats away valuable phone minutes. Even if an appointment is scheduled, what are the chances she actually makes either appointment while having to deal with food, transportation, diapers, and childcare? Not likely—and not due to lack of love or desire.

The reality in poverty is that scarce resources and the need to prioritize utilization of resources is a way of life. What is more important? A well visit for me or my child—or diapers? Another example: What is more important? Going to work to get paid or a well-baby visit, missing work, not getting paid, maybe getting fired, and having even less money? Short-term management of limited resources is a critical and well-honed skill set for the poor.

Yet the response (including mine) of the health professionals, when seeing the deplorable well-visit statistics, is astonishment: "See, even when it's free, they don't come!" I had come face to face with my own intolerance.

This is the character-flaw mentality. Lacking any consideration of circumstances, one creates a false lens of an uncaring mother. This lens breeds shame for those in need and judgment even among those entrusted to care for them.

Let me tell you the story about Maria. I met her in Kauai, Hawaii, while speaking at a local church. Our listeners were very diverse: community and government leaders together with parishioners, reentering citizens, and others in need. After the presentation Maria shared her story with me.

A native Hawaiian, Maria was raised in an upper-middle-class home. She followed her dream to be a social worker, went to college and graduate school, and landed her first job. New to the field and very inexperienced, Maria complained to her supervisor that her clients were habitually late: "If I can be here on time, 'they' should be too," she said.

Maria's supervisor listened and asked Maria to come to the office at 5 a.m. the next morning for a special assignment. When Maria arrived, her supervisor drove her to a very poor area in Kauai, took her purse and money, and told her to be to work at 9 a.m. Maria's experience of having to beg for money at Starbucks, even dressed as a professional, not a beggar, changed everything. Struggling to pay for and find transportation opened her eyes. Just this one aspect of poverty, reliable transportation, was a game changer. Maria quickly realized, just in those few hours, that living in poverty makes everything more difficult. She also felt, for the first time, the embarrassment and stigma that come with asking for help.

Hard times hit the suburbs

Back on the mainland, 2013 was a very rough time for the U.S. economy and devastating for Detroit. With the struggles of the auto industry, hard times hit even the suburbs.

That year I was in line at a West Bloomfield superstore: everything you could possibly want at discount prices, 24/7. It was located in a diverse, upper-middle-class neighborhood, approximately 35 minutes (no traffic) from downtown Detroit. Up until that time I had not witnessed poverty of any kind in my neighborhood.

In line in front of me was a young woman, well-dressed, probably in her 30s. She and her young son, maybe 6 years old, were checked out and ready to pay. She was told that her food vouchers would not cover certain items, and she would either have to pay for them or remove some items. The cashier's voice was loud; her expression was irritated and impatient.

The woman's embarrassment was palpable as she went through her items. But it was the boy who captured my attention. He looked down, putting his head on the conveyor and physically seemed to shrivel. He covered his face with his shirt. I had never seen the shame of poverty so blatant, especially in one so young. This child was being victimized by a society that shames even innocent children needing help. It pained my heart. Is this who we want to be as individuals, communities, and country?

According to an April 2015 *Washington Post* story,

> In the United States tax breaks for lunches eaten on business trips are rarely given the same amount of scrutiny as the use of food stamps at the grocery store, but the ultimate cost to the government is the same.[50]

The character-flaw mentality is a core barrier to changing this nation's system of care for the poor. If we are to succeed, we must change our assumptions, as well as confront the false narrative that the poor are lazy, want to take advantage of the system, and want to be on the dole. We must overcome the belief that before we give someone a safe place to live and food to eat they have to stop drinking or using drugs.

Caring for the poor who are ill must not be conditional—not just because it's the right thing to do clinically, emotionally, and spiritually but because it simply makes sense. A Colorado study found that the average homeless person costs the state $43,000 a year, while housing that person would cost just $17,000 annually.[51]

Once a homeless individual is in stable housing, real recovery becomes much more realistic.

Salt Lake City, Utah, cut its chronic homelessness rate dramatically the last 10 years by giving homeless people permanent places to live, with lots of support services and counseling on site. Starting with a homeless population of 3,000, Salt Lake City recently had reduced that number to 400.[52]

The pervasive attitude that the poor are less—less deserving, less important, with circumstances of their own making—is demonstrated every day in our society. In reality, though, earnings from a full-time, year-round job at minimum wage in Michigan will not lift a single-parent family of three above the poverty level. It simply isn't possible. *By comparison, in 1979 a full-time minimum paying job would lift a family of four out of poverty.*[53]

This phenomenon is true in most states across the country. Minimum wage in the 1960s and 1970s was close to a living wage, barely able to sustain an individual or family, but, according to a 2015 report by the Pew Research Center, that changed starting in the 1980s and has only gotten worse.[54] Wages that do not constitute a living wage are a direct and deep-seated root cause of poverty. Forty-eight million people in this country are not lazy.

Increasing numbers of children and families are living in poverty because the minimum wage has failed to keep pace with the cost of living. As manufacturing jobs have disappeared, replaced with lower-paying service jobs, many more families have fallen into poverty, not out of preference, laziness, or a strategic plan to take advantage of the system. It is the simple economics of survival. When the least educated and least skilled are positioned to live in poverty, their children also are then inclined toward poverty. When nearly 45% of children in this country live in poverty[55] and almost three-quarters of single-mother families with children live in poverty,[56] this is the shaming of a nation and its policies, not its people.

As I write this, the water disaster in Flint, Michigan, is headline news. The voices of the poor—that the water was tainted—were all but ignored by a government determined to solve budget problems. Would it have been different had this occurred in wealthy, mostly white Bloomfield Hills instead of Flint? Yes, this was a case of "environmental injustice" against Flint's largely African American population. That was the conclusion of the Michigan governor's independent task force appointed to investigate the Flint water crisis.[57]

Not until an independent, privately funded scientist publicly demonstrated high levels of lead in Flint's drinking water was the issue brought to national attention. With a destroyed water system in Flint—and lead seeping into the water—the federal government initially offered $5 million to address a multi-million-dollar health crisis.

Meanwhile, the long-term health conditions of the primarily poor residents of Flint remain unknown. If another country had poisoned our water supply and damaged thousands of people, including children, in the process, the United States would likely retaliate with a vengeance. These same crimes against our own people, tragically, were met at first with "politics as usual."

A 'caste system' in the United States

The U.S. caste system is based upon a framework long established. Those living in the communities with the most money get the best education, healthcare, housing, transportation, parks, recreation, police protection, and jobs to sustain them in an era when we know that those with the least need the most. This caste system sends a powerful and painful message to this country's impoverished children and families: "You do not matter."

I hear so often ... "They have no respect for life; look how they kill each other." The statistics are indeed sobering and abysmal. Death rates vary dramatically by race. African American youths are much more likely than their white counterparts to die young. Eight times as many African American youths in Michigan died due to homicide as their white peers in 2012: a total of 68 deaths versus seven among white youths.[58]

I have pondered this question, realizing that our children are reflecting back to us just as we have taught them. What do children learn about their value in society when they often go to bed hungry? What do they learn when their surroundings are dangerous—and even going outside is taking their life into their hands? What do children learn when their school has leaking roofs, rodents, and antiquated books? What message is sent when our system allows entire families to be homeless, hungry, without basic needs, with inferior education, in crime-ridden and rat-infested neighborhoods, with substandard housing, and young men having a better chance of going to prison than college?

Just what do our children learn when they watch TV and see how the other side of America lives? Do they feel important? Valued? Respected? What is society saying to our children living in poverty? The message, unfortunately, is all too clear: "You are not important."

When children feel that their life is unimportant, know that they are not valued by society, and learn that their future is bleak—because we as a society do not respect their lives—how do they learn to value life? Our children usually learn exactly what we teach them. Sadly, the value of life too often is determined by the size of one's pocketbook and the color of one's skin.

As actions speak louder than words, the pervasive message—in both word and deed—in this country is all too clear: The poor are not important.

Chapter 6

The Health Connection

Peeling back the onion

So here we are in the poorest city in the country, at a struggling not for profit, with thousands of poor people in need, 400 workers counting on Matrix for employment, a regular salary, and healthcare. I am overwhelmed with the demands, the barriers, and the failing health of this wonderful organization.

The response from banks, funders, vendors, and my not-for-profit brothers and sisters was, by and large, discouraging. We learned very quickly that "crisis marketing"—asking for help to sustain a failing not for profit, even one with 100 years of service—has little appeal to donors or funders.

Seventy years earlier my family had received services at Casa Maria, an after-school program for kids living in Southwest Detroit. Sports, tutoring, snacks, a safe place. Now a corrupt city government cut our funding, and with very little money from any other source, Casa Maria was about to be shuttered. Our last desperate measure was an urgent letter to our donors: "Please give. Without your help, these doors will be closing!"

This was like gambling on the horses, no matter how adorable, no matter how compelling the story ... no one likes to bet on a loser. Even though we sent out hundreds of letters to those who had supported us in years gone by, we received less than a thousand dollars. The begging (I mean the fund-development) experts are right: People don't want to donate to a lost cause. After a good fight, with no stone left unturned, Casa Maria closed after many decades of service to the community. This was a failure, painful both professionally and personally.

The Casa Maria experience led to a new communications approach, aptly coined by our CFO "lipstick on a pig." Although the reality was that Matrix was essentially destitute, we found several positive nuggets, mostly clinical (e.g., documented immunization rates, home-care services to shut-ins, improved grades in school), to promote a successful public image. Like flashing a faux designer bag when one can't afford the real thing, we pretended. The lipstick gave us a sense of hope, some much needed pride. And it brought in donations—not to save Casa Maria but to support the larger Matrix effort.

These were tough lessons we were learning. As noted, donors seldom give to organizations on the brink, and banks usually don't extend credit to organizations or individuals who need it most. We owed money to everyone. Each day was like an onion, with every peel yet another layer of problems and debt. The day I realized we owed the Federal Pension Bureau over a hundred thousand dollars (as a result of past mismanagement of the organization's pension fund) I felt the walls closing in.

All we could focus on was survival, payroll to payroll, cutting costs wherever we could (switching to white vinegar as our primary cleaning solvent), turning down thermostats, balancing bill payments, loathing creditor calls, and negotiating reduced paybacks. Just when we could see light at the end of the tunnel, a broken pipe, a leaky roof, or a dreaded and incredibly expensive (and infuriating) bedbug infestation would strike and again set us back.

Our inability to support ourselves financially was affecting every aspect of our existence. I had trouble sleeping. The responsibility for the organization—hundreds of employees and thousands of clients in need—was increasingly overwhelming. Our organization was struggling ... just as our clients were. The irony was not lost on me. Imagine living like this for a lifetime. Imagine if it were my children, not my employees. Bottom line: Our management team felt immense responsibility and didn't want to let down individuals or the community.

The fire

Then I got the call. Our building on Warren Avenue, the recently evacuated office for our Walter Reuther Senior Services Program, was on fire. I knew the building, part of a small mall of three businesses. Our neighbors, the shuttered businesses on either side of us (a candy store and a shoe store), had since long abandoned the area. Subsequently those vacant storefronts served as a self-made homeless refuge—even without water and electricity (and *with* rodents).

Just days before the fire I had relocated staff and closed the building. Black mold permeated the ceiling and walls, not to mention the overall decrepit condition of the building. I found it odd, even amid the terrible conditions, that some of the workers resisted the move to an improved but still dilapidated location. Work imitating life. Ironic.

I arrived on site to find Detroit's firefighters hosing our building. I sought out the man in charge. It was sunny, beautiful spring day and, thankfully, no one had been in the sprawling structure. I too excitedly asked, "Is it totaled?" He replied, "No, it's not a total loss." My disappointment was apparent. He asked to look in my trunk! No, I did not set the fire, but I did realize that the fire would provide an insurance claim on a building I had no intent of refurbishing. The fire and the eventual insurance check seemed like divine intervention.

Even with the building boarded up, thieves within hours would strip every last piece of scrap, every piece of plumbing. Hours after it was re-boarded, thieves would return to strip some more. Seems our good karma, a burnt and abandoned building, had a ripple effect of good fortune for others struggling to survive. Within days, the air-conditioning unit off the roof was stolen. Another insurance claim and another check to keep our collective head above water. I had never done business this way. It was all legal, but I had never before "worked the system" as a survival strategy.

I learned firsthand that the ruined building on Warren Avenue—like the city around it, the charity it once represented, and the very clients we were serving—was sick and dying. No one seemed to care. Our donors, our banks, our community, our government, other not for profits, our vendors, and the corporate community … no one.

The relocation of our Senior Services Program from the now-burnt building required notification to the Detroit Area Agency on Aging (DAAA). I knew of the organization, and I knew it funded the Matrix senior program. DAAA's CEO, Paul Bridgewater, a longstanding leader in Detroit, sent me a report, "Dying Before Their Time."[59] "Read this," he said. I did.

I was not prepared. This report hit me between the eyes. As noted in Chapter 3, I learned that in Detroit our seniors, ages 50–59, were sicker and dying at a rate 122% higher than their counterparts in Michigan. How could this be? In America, just 35 minutes from my own home in the suburbs. But I knew it was true.

Since I had started at Matrix a year before, my eyes had been witnessing what the report was revealing. Poor seniors, the majority African American, often have to choose between food and medicine, struggle to get to their doctor appointments, and have no dependable transportation. Then there are the bus drivers who frequently drive right by seniors waiting in their wheelchairs, thereby avoiding the delay and extra effort it takes to load them onto the bus.

Our support of meals, chore services, and companionship, so appreciated by our clients, was paltry response at best. We were virtually the only connection to society for some of our homebound seniors. Funding from the United Auto Workers, a staple for this program, was based on a dwindling but generous UAW membership. Each year, however, there was less funding, each year less service, each year seniors dying before their time. I came to realize that the poverty/health connection was irrefutable.

The poverty/health connection

Once you start looking, the evidence is abundant that poverty takes a terrible toll on one's health. Several cases in point:

- "Today, as health-insurance companies are faced with 70 million Medicaid enrollees, the poverty/health connection is front and center. Economic hardship is consistently associated with poorer education and health outcomes."[60]

- "The consequences of poor nutrition or devastating food insecurity for older Americans make them 60% more likely to experience depression and over 50% more likely to suffer heart attacks."[61]

Not just in Detroit but nationally, the causal relationship between poverty and health is both compelling and convincing.

- According to *The Washington Post* (April 9, 2015), "Premature death for women in the U.S. is about on par with Mexico, which spends just $858 on health care per capita, compared with nearly $8,000 per capita in the U.S."[62]

Health Disparities for Those Living in Poverty

Poverty status is based on Gallup's best estimate of those in poverty, according to the U.S. Census Bureau's 2011 thresholds.

	Percentage with Disease in Poverty	Percentage with Disease Not in Poverty	Difference (Percentage Points)
Depression	30.9	15.8	15.1
Asthma	17.1	11.0	6.1
Obesity	31.8	26.0	5.8
Diabetes	14.8	10.1	4.7
High blood pressure	31.8	29.1	2.7
Heart attack	5.8	3.8	2.0
Cancer	6.3	7.1	-0.8
High cholesterol	25.0	26.0	-1.0

Source: Gallup Healthways Well-Being Index, 2011   © 2016 Transition To Success®

- Living on incomes less than 200% of the federal poverty level claimed more than 400 million quality-adjusted life years between 1997 and 2002, meaning that poverty had a larger impact on Americans' health than tobacco use and obesity combined.[63]

- If that isn't disturbing enough, brain development is negatively impacted when children experience poverty and specifically food insecurity, even low levels on an intermittent basis. And as indicated in Chapter 3, such food insecurity directly affects the development of children's brains.

- Emerging research suggests that living in poverty also may negatively affect the development of important connections between/among critical parts of the brain.[64]

- Research by Children's Health Launch has shown that, compared with young children who have plenty of nutritious food to eat, children under age 3 in "food-insecure families are more likely to have a history of hospitalizations, be in fair or poor health, be at risk for developmental delays, and have iron-deficiency anemia."[65]

I was running the largest Head Start program in Detroit. I witnessed child hunger and families with children living in poverty every day. Not like you see in the commercials, not the pictures of almost naked children with bulging stomachs ... this was different: camouflaged, yet visible when looking. It was hitting me hard, often when I least expected it.

Happy holidays

Angel Tree was a new holiday tradition at Matrix. Employees and donors accept wish lists from clients, complete the shopping, and wrap the gifts. The Saturday before the holiday our event would bring the two together: families with children and donors for a shared holiday meal, music, Santa, and all the festivities. Staff loved the event, donors reveled in the real connections, and the response from families was very positive.

My first holiday at Matrix and the Matrix Center (previously called Mt. Zion Lutheran Church) was alive. Decorations, holiday lights, stacks of beautifully wrapped presents, children running around everywhere, music, photos with Santa ... the spirit of the season was alive! I personally greeted each arrival at the door.

I lean over to be at eye level with a little girl, maybe 4 or 5, hair beautifully done, in her holiday dress. Before I can say a word, she looks directly at me, and her sad eyes speak clearly: Something is wrong ... "Is there food here?" she whispers. My heart aches to hear this question. I whisper back, "Yes, honey, there is lots of food. Your mom will take you to it." She then asks, "Is there juice too? Can we take some home?" I'm taken aback. "Yes, I will make sure you take some home." Her mother, hearing what her daughter was asking, is embarrassed. No one else hears our hushed conversation.

We connected. She saw my tears forming, and I saw hers. Another moment in time that changed me forever.

I continued to be faced with the raw reality that children who don't get enough to eat can have trauma and lifelong consequences. Consequences that impact their ability to learn, to cope, to feel safe, to reach their full potential. Consequences that change the trajectory of their lives. In the United States, one of the richest countries in the world, more than one in five children is food-insecure.[66]

In my world 1,300 little people, ages 3 to 5, are in our care every day in the poorest city in the nation. Hungry children cannot happen on my watch. My blissful ignorance had now borne witness to the poor being sicker, dying younger, and suffering with basic needs going unmet—and I was playing a leading role in the unfolding tragedy.

I will never forget that little girl or her mother. Their pain left an indelible mark on my heart. More importantly, they fueled my determination to do something about it.

The role of environment

According to the *Professional Guide to Diseases,*

> Human interaction with environment starts at conception and continues throughout life until the very moment of death, clearly influencing health and disease in many ways. No part of the person's environment can be strictly divorced from any other aspect.[67]

Poverty forces its casualties to live under stressful, traumatic, and sometimes fatal conditions. Even the healthiest among us who come in contact with toxins will become ill. Adding insult to injury, economic status often determines the amount and quality of healthcare that people have access to—for themselves and their families—in the United States.

As I sit here today writing this book, I receive a call from a man leading the initiative to bring water to the residents of Flint. His frustrations are apparent, particularly regarding the lead-poisoning health crisis. I ask him, "How many children do we think have been poisoned by lead in Flint?" His reply: "We think around 8,000."

Eight thousand children whose lives are now impacted forever.

Lead poisoning: caused completely by exposure to environmental conditions with absolutely no genetic predisposition; causes long-term neurological damage. Lead requires immediate medical attention, all covered under health insurance, all treated by national standards and protocols. Lead poisoning is an environmentally based medical condition.

Everyone has seen the commercials: "If you or anyone in your family has been exposed to asbestos, call us now. You may be eligible for compensation." If you watch TV, you know that exposure to asbestos causes an often-fatal form of cancer called mesothelioma, which has no genetic predisposition. It can be caused only by exposure— environmental exposure to asbestos.

HIV-AIDS has no genetic predisposition, Lyme disease has no genetic predisposition, the Zika virus has no genetic predisposition. Yet all of these and so many more are recognized, researched, treated, and paid for by the healthcare industry ... and appropriately so. Just as these conditions are environmentally based, so is poverty.

Poverty is an environmentally based medical condition.

Being exposed to the conditions of poverty makes people sick. The healthcare industry recognizes that exposure to these social determinants is a direct cause of, or exacerbates, many illnesses, yet poverty remains in the Dark Ages, saturated in myths and misconceptions, led by good intentions but immune to the standards of science where research and data drive practice.

Treating poverty, just like treating lead poisoning, as an environmentally based medical condition requires defined-care management services that allow poor children and families to make the transition to improved health and economic self-sufficiency.

When a society has "connective tissue" between and among healthcare, education, government, and human services, along with real treatment planning with advocacy and support, poverty can be treated. Like the treatment of other medical conditions, the treatment of poverty requires continuity, coordination, and comprehensive care. Treating poverty as the medical condition it is will improve both health and the economics for patient, family, community, health plan, and our nation.

Chapter 7

Seeing Nails Everywhere

When you're a hammer, everything looks like a nail. In other words, where you come from greatly influences how you see the world. The actual 1966 quote from U.S. psychologist Abraham Maslow: "I suppose it is tempting, if the only tool you have is a hammer, to treat everything as if it were a nail."[68]

Lessons from the hammers and nails of healthcare

I came from the healthcare field, spending more than 20 years running healthcare-related programs. As a managed-healthcare executive I learned very quickly that, just like not for profits, "No money, no mission." In healthcare, unlike human services, funding streams are fairly consistent, and payment structures are based primarily on the level of illness of your enrollees.

I also learned that, in healthcare, quality is king. It's quite simple. Enrollment drives revenue. To increase enrollment you need to appeal to your potential enrollee market through pricing and your network of providers. Once individuals enroll in your plan, your provider network tries to keep them healthy, thereby reducing the overall cost of care. The goal is a consistent, always growing, enrollment of healthy enrollees. That's how you make money in healthcare.

The industry is continually improving ways to keep its membership healthy by ensuring that, for any given condition (e.g., diabetes, asthma, cancer, etc.), best practices or standards of care are followed by physicians, allied health professionals, and the facilities caring for your membership.

Healthcare, like most other industries, has licensing regulations, accrediting requirements, and defined continuous quality improvement (CQI) processes. These systems are designed to increase quality by identifying faulty elements or areas that need improvement.[69]

This is the world I came from.

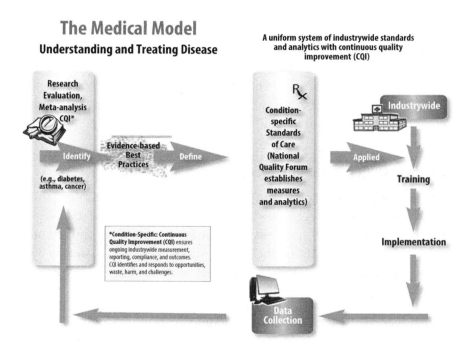

The Medical Model
Understanding and Treating Disease

A uniform system of industrywide standards and analytics with continuous quality improvement (CQI)

Research Evaluation, Meta-analysis CQI*

Identify

(e.g., diabetes, asthma, cancer)

Evidence-based Best Practices

Define

Condition-specific Standards of Care (National Quality Forum establishes measures and analytics)

R_x

Industrywide

Applied

Training

Implementation

*Condition-Specific: Continuous Quality Improvement (CQI) ensures ongoing industrywide measurement, reporting, compliance, and outcomes. CQI identifies and responds to opportunities, waste, harm, and challenges.

Data Collection

At upper left in the preceding chart are volumes of research and evaluation for any particular condition—e.g., diabetes. As you can imagine, medical research covers virtually every condition, from thousands of sources. In 2015 more than 1 million papers on bioscience were published.[70] We do not expect practicing physicians to read all the research and self-determine which practices they will follow. Physicians are closely guided by industry leaders who identify evidence-based best practices, then publish and promote standards of care that health providers are expected to follow. With training, then implementation, healthcare has consistency of methodologies and protocols across practitioners.

For example, years ago the research told us that nutrition services can improve outcomes for diabetic patients. The data were clear: Registered dietitians can augment and complement physician care by preventing, assessing, and treating nutritional problems in diabetics. Today a physician referral to the dietitian is a required standard protocol for newly diagnosed diabetic patients.

Accrediting agencies like the Joint Commission on Accreditation of Healthcare Organizations/National Committee for Quality Assurance (JCAHO/NCQA) and health plans monitor compliance with this standard. Failure to follow industry standards in the treatment of a medical condition will likely result in the physician being cited for noncompliance, potential nonpayment for service, and possible loss of accreditations.[71]

As outcome data are collected for the condition, the data are integrated with the newest research and evaluation to evolve the next iteration of the standard. This process, CQI, ensures ongoing industrywide research, evaluation, measurement, reporting, compliance, outcomes, and identification and response to opportunities to improve those outcomes. The intent of the process also is to minimize waste and harm, as well as to address challenges.

CQI is why, as recently as 25 years ago, amputations for diabetics were fairly common, but today amputations for diabetics are considered exceptions. CQI improves quality of care, quality of life for patients, and the bottom line for the health plan. CQI is a win-win-win! Found in virtually every industry, the process to continually improve what we do is accomplished when research and outcomes drive practice.

A brief, personal case study

The consistency in the healthcare-delivery system was demonstrated in yet another one of my unscientific experiments. In 2003 my dad was diagnosed with dementia. He and my mother could no longer live independently, and they came to live with me. First order of business: getting dad evaluated and determining the treatment plan. Starting with my primary-care physician, we were referred to a series of specialists who ordered numerous tests. The care manager, a nurse, helped with every aspect of my father's care, ensuring we had access and understood every step of his treatment and all the medications he was prescribed.

Although our actual time with physicians was minimal, the team of nurses, allied health professionals, and staff were wonderful, guiding us every step of the way, including information on community supports not connected with the healthcare system. Although my father's condition was chronic and lifelong, the medications were making a huge difference in his mood, his ability to sleep, and even some noted improvement in his memory. Better living through chemistry was never more apparent.

Six months after the diagnosis my parents decided to live with my brother in a rural area of North Carolina. In North Carolina, Dad was taken to another large healthcare system for his workup. So that we as adult children could get an independent evaluation, his records from Michigan were not sent to North Carolina. Would the diagnosis be the same? The meds? The tests?

Other than one slight change of a single medication for his diabetes, the process, tests, and meds were all the same, including the referral to community support resources. The faces changed, the facilities changed, but the treatment protocols were all the same.

Healthcare, unlike human services, is not necessarily driven by good intentions. Healthcare is based on science. Like most other industries, research and data drive practice. In healthcare, standards of care apply to illnesses caused by genetic predisposition (e.g., colon cancer), illnesses caused by environmental exposures (e.g., lead poisoning), and illnesses caused by trauma (e.g., broken leg). Regardless of the cause, the healthcare field has diagnoses, guidelines, treatment protocols, billing, analytics, and the ongoing process of CQI.

There can be no dispute: Healthcare responds to genetic disease, environmentally based conditions, and trauma-induced injury. Even when the condition is caused by a mosquito or deer tick, the medical community responds. All three types of conditions are treated with uniform, standardized protocols of practice.

A key premise of this book is that poverty is an environmentally based condition. A second premise is that exposure to environmental conditions, including toxins like lead paint in substandard housing and the social determinants of health like lack of food (see ensuing section), makes people sick. Understanding poverty as an environmentally based treatable condition stops the blame/shame game because poverty is not about who you are, it's about where you live and your social/environmental exposures.

Treating Evironmentally Based, Industry-Accepted Medical Conditions*

Enviornmental Exposures	Symptoms
Lead ingestion	Irritability, high blood pressure, long-term neurological damage
Asbestos	Trouble breathing, nausea, vomiting
Mosquito bites	Fever, rash, joint pain, conjunctivitis, muscle pain, headache
Limited access to fresh fruits, vegetables, and exercise	Increased thirst, blurred vision
Cigarette smoking and secondhand smoke	Wheezing, increased risk of cancer, asthma, COPD
Accidents	Broken bones, closed head injuries
Pollution	Difficulty breathing, decrease in lung function, wheezing
Social Determinants of Health Food insecurity, high crime rates, inadequate/unaffordable housing, lack of access to basic resources, limited access to quality healthcare and transportation, poorly performing schools, racism, unemployment, and underemployment	Increased rates of diabetes and high blood pressure, infant and maternal mortality, increased depression and mental health disorders, asthma, compromised immune system and brain development, higher death rates

*Note: Recognized disease without genetic predisposition

Diagnosis	Standard of Care	Billable
Lead poisoning	Required	✓
Cancer/ mesothelioma	Required	✓
Zika, West Nile, yellow fever, and malaria viruses	Required	✓
Type II diabetes Obesity	Required	✓
Nicotine addiction	Required	✓
Trauma	Required	✓
Asthma/COPD	Required	✓
Extreme poverty (ICD 10 VZ59.5)	Transition To Success®	Some state Medicaid plans and Medicare for chronic conditions Care Management (CPT 99490)

© 2016 Transition To Success®

The United States healthcare industry has, since its inception, treated genetics-based, environmentally based, and trauma-based medical conditions. Exposure leads to symptoms, then to diagnosis. Standards of care are applied, and claims are submitted for reimbursement. Even sexually transmitted diseases, stigma and all, are recognized, treated, and reimbursed by the medical industry.

It's time to treat poverty the same way.

The social determinants of health

It's not news. As indicated in the preceding diagram, environmental conditions can make people sick. Enter the social determinants of health. The social determinants of health are defined as the "conditions in which people are born, grow, work, and age. These circumstances are shaped by the distribution of money, power, and resources at global, national, and local levels."[72]

When an individual, regardless of age, race, religion, and culture is exposed to these social determinants of health—racism, food insecurity, high crime rates, poorly performing schools, unemployment, underemployment, inadequate/unaffordable housing, lack of access to basic resources (clean water: case in point, Flint), limited access to quality healthcare and transportation—statistically speaking they will be sicker, cost more, and die younger.

These environmental exposures lead to increased rates of diabetes and high blood pressure, infant and maternal mortality, depression, mental health disorders, asthma, compromised immune system and brain development, and higher death rates. Even though poverty is recognized in healthcare with its own diagnostic code, it is not billable. Understandably so, given the fact that there are (as yet!) no agreed-upon protocols or guidelines for treating it. Therein lies the rub.

Poverty can be treated within existing Medicaid benefits by using appropriate billable mental-health codes (e.g., Adjustment Reaction). Unfortunately, this indirect treatment and billing pathway tends to reinforce the character-flaw mentality. In reality *being* poor often contributes toward making individuals mentally and physically unhealthy. In short, poverty requires treatment.

Additionally, we learn from industry experts ...

- More than four of five physicians surveyed (85%) say social needs result in worse health. More than four of five doctors (85%) also say patients' social needs are as important as their medical conditions.[73]

- The American Academy of Pediatrics, recognizing this direct relationship, now recommends that pediatricians screen for poverty to help eliminate its toxic health effects.[74]

- Researchers Paula Braverman and Laura Gottlieb report: "A large and compelling body of evidence has been accumulated, particularly during the last two decades, that reveals a powerful role for social factors—apart from medical care—in shaping health across a wide range of health indicators, settings and populations."[75]

- Jamal et al., studying 2001 U.S. death data, conclude that "potentially avoidable factors associated with lower educational status account for almost half of all deaths among work.ing age adults in the U.S."[76]

The time has come to recognize that the individual's ability to meet basic social needs are directly connected to the health of America—not only of those in poverty but, indeed, of the nation itself.

Chapter 8

Raise Your Hand if You
Want to Be Poor

'Poverty is not an accident'

When I arrived at Matrix in 2006, almost everywhere I looked I saw a hand-out mentality, not a hand-up mentality. Michelle's powerful statement, "People want to get better; they just don't know how," never left me. I learned very quickly that no one wants to be poor.

I have asked thousands of people in the course of my work and hundreds of speeches. "Who wants to be poor?" No one ever raises their hand. I ask, "Who wants their children to be poor?" Again, no one ever raises their hand. Not once. Ever. So if no one wants to be poor, why was it that when I looked at the Matrix system, the system in Detroit, and the system across this country the success stories were few and far between. I had no idea how to treat poverty. It seemed an enigma, an age-old social problem, a fact of life.

The words of South African President (1994–99) Nelson Mandela inspired me: "Like slavery and apartheid, poverty is not natural. It is man-made, and it can be overcome and eradicated by the actions of human beings."

I began my exploration into not just understanding poverty but defining how to treat the condition of poverty. I was in fairly close contact with 10,000 poor people of all ages, colors, races, cultures, religions, and backgrounds—and not one of them wanted to be poor.

My search for solutions began.

I could not find statistics or industry standards that demonstrated how we in the United States were doing in this regard. I found plenty of stats on how most poor people in America were doing, but almost nothing on how many adults, children, families, or special populations were moving out of poverty and, most importantly, how they were doing it. I learned very quickly that the absence of this information was true not only at Matrix, but throughout the entire delivery system in every region of the country.

I found this to be the current "poverty paradigm" of research, evaluation, and practice in the United States.

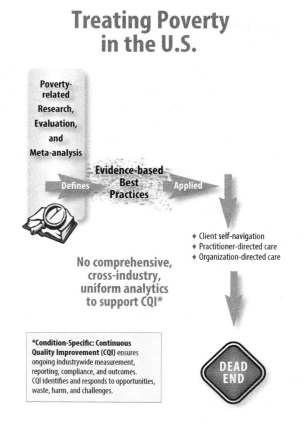

Treating Poverty in the U.S.

Poverty-related Research, Evaluation, and Meta-analysis

Defines

Evidence-based Best Practices

Applied

♦ Client self-navigation
♦ Practitioner-directed care
♦ Organization-directed care

No comprehensive, cross-industry, uniform analytics to support CQI*

*Condition-Specific: Continuous Quality Improvement (CQI) ensures ongoing industrywide measurement, reporting, compliance, and outcomes. CQI identifies and responds to opportunities, waste, harm, and challenges.

DEAD END

© 2016 Transition To Success®

The preceding diagram represents the basic framework for understanding and dealing with poverty in the U.S.

On the left is poverty-related research. Initially I was overwhelmed but encouraged. Millions of pages of information, research, evaluation, and studies across healthcare, human services, education, faith-based entities, and government programs. All dedicated to understanding poverty. Some of it awesome, some of it not so much.

The comprehensive and extensive body of research led to researchers identifying evidence-based best practices for poverty, based on statistically significant results. This, however, is where the process seemed to hit a wall.

The next phase of my journey was beginning.

The wall

Unlike the treatment of medical conditions, or even most industry processes, there are no uniform analytics, uniform standard protocols, or overseeing entities identifying best practices for this industry. I found no systematic standards of care to treat the environmentally based medical condition of poverty. I found an industry rich in good intentions supported by reams of very expensive but disconnected research.

I realized that the consequences of treating poverty in a complex delivery system oblivious to the science of continuous quality improvement (CQI) are devastating—both clinically to the human condition and fiscally for a nation. America is paying a high price for regularly unsuccessful attempts to care for those in need.

In the existing system to treat poverty in the United States, clients with the fewest resources—limited access to phones, transportation, and computers, and many with limited ability to read—are expected to self-navigate not just one complex system but four systems: healthcare, human services, government, and education services.

This is analogous to telling our diabetic patient, "I'm sorry, you have diabetes, go figure it out, decide on your own what specialists you should see, what tests you need, and how to manage your condition." That, of course, would be patently ridiculous. Healthcare professionals would never do this because the cost and quality of healthcare would be significantly compromised.

In healthcare the more complex your condition, the more resources you're provided, even if your disease was your own fault (e.g., nicotine-induced lung cancer) or exacerbated by your behavior. Even the non-compliant patient receives care.

My sister was the life of the party. She died very young, at age 47. Her death was caused by complications from diabetes. She was a seriously noncompliant patient—simply unable or unwilling, for whatever reasons, to follow the diet and exercise regimens the disease requires. The complexities of her physical and psychological condition went far beyond my understanding. But I do know this: The sicker my sister became, the more resources her health plan made available. She had myriad physicians, care managers, home care, telephone supports, dietitians, and machines to monitor sugar and weigh food.

Although I'm certain her life was extended by the intensive care she received, her inability (and some would say unwillingness) to manage her condition resulted in her premature death. The management of her care by the health professionals entrusted with that care was comprehensive, as was the healthcare coverage afforded her by her husband's employer, General Motors.

At no time was my sister ever expected to self-navigate her course of care or support services. At every turn she received guidance. Her physicians, nurse care managers, and allied health professionals directed and provided the best treatment available, just like it's done for thousands of other diabetics in this country. My sister's care was closely monitored and directed; she was supported despite her blatant noncompliance.

In poverty we expect that the most at-risk individuals will navigate complex systems of healthcare, human services, government services, and education—each with varying requirements, qualifications, and means testing, using limited phone minutes, inability or limited ability to read and write, limited and/or unreliable bus and transportation services to get to a disconnected array of services in disparate locations, with long lines in dirty and worn-out buildings that have hours designed not for the customers but for the people who work there. A Head Start program that starts at 8:30 a.m. and has no childcare offered before or after school is not designed to promote employment for the working poor. Yet that is a common scenario across our country and an ongoing battle we eventually lost in Detroit.

Practitioner-directed care

The second consequence of our current paradigm for treating poverty is practitioner-directed care. Imagine if we allowed all physicians, individually, to pick and choose what treatment they would apply to any and every condition based on their own review and understanding (or lack thereof) regarding the research, based on what they think will work, or what is easiest, or least expensive—or simply based on their good intentions.

Imagine the chaos that would ensue. Also imagine the deterioration of patient care, the impact on our ability to understand what works and what doesn't, the increased expense. Yet this is how practitioners in the human services and related industries operate. We are told what forms to fill out, where to send them, how many copies to keep, who can get service and, most importantly, who is excluded from service. Yet in terms of how to treat the actual condition of poverty, there is no industry standard. Good intentions, while plentiful, do not constitute protocols.

Organization-directed care

The third consequence of lack of standardization in the treatment of poverty is organization-directed care. Imagine if we allowed each hospital to self-determine how it would manage infectious disease or contaminated materials, with workers at each hospital doing whatever they wanted based on their own opinions or willingness to bear expense. Imagine the public health risk.

In healthcare, licensing and accreditation requirements ensure adherence to organizational protocols to protect health, safety of patients, staff, and community. The healthcare delivery system enforces uniform practices and measurements for patients, practitioners, and providers—not just in the management of the services but, more importantly, in the treatment of the condition. If the protocols aren't followed, healthcare organizations face nonpayment or worse: loss of license or accreditation.

In poverty, clients self-direct, practitioners self-direct, and organizations self-determine. This chaotic, complex, siloed delivery system of care does not, on any level, integrate CQI. Unlike nearly all other industries and endeavors in society, the treatment of poverty does not use data and research to drive practice. Rather the industry is fueled by good intentions—$1.6 trillion worth of good intentions for 70 million Medicaid enrollees and 48 million people living in poverty. Good intentions and money do not replace continuous quality improvement.

CQI—the process of improvement through the standardization of procedures, processes, delivery, and analytics—is not new. Across industry and management, manufacturing, aeronautics, sports, library science, even car-maintenance schedules … protocols are designed to be consistently applied.

Why not in the treatment of poverty?

Chapter 9

Where There's Hope, There's Life

Finding pathways out of poverty

The reality I discovered in my search was that demonstrated pathways for helping to move people out of poverty simply did not exist. If they did, I had trouble locating them. I felt I had to wing it. Matrix programs were running with a bleak fiscal picture, but they no longer were on life support. I needed to know what moves people out of poverty, and I needed something now.

After more than 20 years in healthcare, I knew that care management, essential in healthcare, improves quality and decreases costs.

At Matrix our system for coordinating care was haphazard at best and overall was missing a critical component. The current system of care for a person living in poverty depends almost entirely on the personal knowledge and capabilities of the practitioner the customer happens to connect with.

Across the organization, across our community, and across the country, there was little consistency in practice, data collection, or evaluation. Clinical decision making in poverty is highly variable because the cases involving clients are diverse and complex.

In March 2013 at 3:30 in the afternoon a 24-year-old woman and a 5-year-old girl were dropped off at Matrix, sent by taxi by another human-services organization a few miles away. "They told me to come here," the woman said. At this administrative office I was the only clinician on site. Since this wasn't the first time a homeless person had come through our doors, Miss Shirley, the office manager, knew exactly what to do; she began collecting snacks and fruit from the staff. I welcomed the pair into my office, and the little girl spoke first: "We're hungry." The food arrived and was placed in front of this pretty little girl. She quickly divided the snacks into four piles, as equal as possible. She announced with authority, "OK, we each get some now, and we save the rest for dinner." The mother, without eye contact, nodded. Both began eating their designated portions.

I suddenly realized that this little child was caring for her mother more effectively than anyone else in their world. Sometimes I wish my heart could forget what my eyes have seen.

Over the course of 12 months this young mother, struggling with both mental health and substance abuse, had been in touch with no fewer than 10 organizations, each with some level of responsibility for her and/or her daughter's care. They included the Department of Human Services, community mental health, Head Start, Medicaid, a local pediatrician, a community health provider, a hospital emergency room, a public school enrollment into kindergarten, City of Detroit Substance Abuse Services, several local human-services organizations, and now Matrix. All of us … yet here she was (with her little girl), mentally ill, drug-addicted, homeless, and hungry.

Each of these organizations, critical to protect the lives of our most vulnerable, failed. At no time in the delivery were decisive action and responsibility taken. Yet I'm sure each did what it could, what it thought it was supposed to.

This woman, like the system of care designed to support her, was unable to identify, organize, coordinate, or respond to her complex needs and corresponding care. Tragically, her daughter's life, statistically, also was hanging in the balance.

Studies on welfare-to-work programs indicate that successful engagement strategies include a high degree of case management that begins with intake.[77]

Initial comprehensive assessments are critical to identify immediate service needs, determine the capabilities and capacities of participants, and identify any special intensive needs.

The research demonstrating the effectiveness of care management on health was and is substantial. In one comparative effectiveness study of the chronic-care model, family-care integration has significant ability to improve both physical and mental health outcomes for persons with those needs.[78]

It's not rocket science. Common sense tells us that coordinating care improves health, and good physical and mental health is essential to improved economic self-sufficiency. In order to improve the lives of vulnerable populations, we need to identify, coordinate, and access diverse resources across lines of neighborhood, community, social resources, and healthcare, all connected in a multi-directional manner.

With little money, no infrastructure beyond Matrix, and only 2-1-1 technology (a national information and referral system available to 90% of the U.S. population) to support us, Matrix care managers began taking responsibility for making these vital connections. Together with the client, they increasingly accessed resources by calling 2-1-1, thereby identifying all supports and services, then they sorted with the client the best options and next steps.

An emerging strategy

Our emerging strategy: Provide each client with a direct-care professional trained to conduct solution-focused interventions; link referrals; follow up and coach; and guide the customer through life's obstacles—obstacles that create setbacks, not hopelessness. Care management identifies and connects to the available, already-funded programs and services clients need to succeed. Care management teaches empowerment and provides essential supports as clients make the transition, step by step, to a better place, improving their health, their understanding of the effects of poverty, and their economic self-sufficiency. In short, care management holds the community-based delivery system accountable.

At Matrix we began looking at each program, identifying those positions within each program that were currently being used to navigate services (or could be)—not just services at Matrix, but all services funded to support our clients. Care management became a core service in our Partnership for Housing program. True care managers don't just say, "Call 2-1-1." Rather, especially for those most at risk, they ensure that the needed service is accessible. When service delivery hits a barrier, care managers drive the accountability process, bringing in the physician or administration as needed to make sure care is delivered.

With our determination to hold the system accountable and a new culture of "Behavior unchallenged is behavior unchanged," together care managers and administrators went up the chain of command to advocate for people and to access services. This included the Michigan Housing Department: calling, e-mailing, writing, and sending pictures to tell the story of deplorable housing conditions inflicted on our clients by their out-of-state construction and management companies.

The homes were either occupied or identified by the management company as ready to be rented. The well-intentioned vision of the housing plan was to place at-risk families in these government-funded, brand-new dwellings, ensuring that the client was positioned to pay the subsidized rent and associated expenses. Michigan government paid out-of-state construction and management companies to build and manage housing in Detroit. Clients' rent would then be applied toward the eventual purchase of the home. Matrix was to be paid a monthly fee, based on occupancy, by the management company.

Our job was ensuring that eligible women and children were always on standby to fill available homes. Matrix was to be paid monthly to identify and support these single mothers to enhance their potential for success. By maximizing housing-support funding, along with all the other services our clients were eligible for, we set a plan in motion toward economic self-sufficiency. From desperate homelessness to a thriving life and future. But the dream, solid in principle, was a nightmare in practice. I found mothers so afraid of returning to the local shelter that they were willing to live, silently, in sub-standard conditions with their children. We were now their voice.

Months later, after many calls and letters, the state housing director finally came to Detroit, a slew of executives in tow, in a lovely, air-conditioned bus. I had hope. We toured state-funded, dilapidated homes. They took pictures of the slums they had, in effect, created.

They were witnessing firsthand the fact that the companies they paid millions to had built inferior homes; failed to maintain the homes; and failed to pay Matrix, as required, for our support services to the residents. Residents slated to become owners of these homes had renewed hope. But the state housing executives returned to Lansing, promising to take action. We never heard from them again.

Cooperating with local landlords

One by one we moved all our mothers and families out of the deficient government housing units and into livable space, negotiating deals with local landlords looking for stable renters. This was the deal: We will screen your tenants, place your tenants, assist with coordination for applicable housing subsidies, and provide care-management services to your tenants. The landlords' part of the deal: clean, affordable housing and, at end of each month, $100 paid to Matrix.

It worked—and still works. Since 2004, all clients (100%) in the program have had an income level to support their monthly housing costs.[79] Everyone wants decent housing that is affordable. Everyone wants a decent place to live. No one wants to be poor.

For years we hounded the government-funded management companies to pay our fees. With minimal support from the state, eventually we gave up. Legal recourse was not feasible; it costs money. In poverty, for both individuals and organizations, having to deal with bureaucracy without the financial resources to hold the system accountable leads to frustration, anger, and ultimately hopelessness. I discontinued all of our state government-related housing contracts. Instead, care management focused on maximizing Section 8 housing vouchers in partnership with responsible landlords.

In the government's best-laid plans (I suspect with good intentions), corporations receiving millions in government contracts profit on the backs of the poorest and most in need. With the voices of those in poverty silenced, who are the "real" customers in this system?

Partnership for Housing, with coordinated care management (CCM) services to our once-homeless mothers and their children, has proven to be one of the most effective Matrix programs.

Since the program's inception in 2004, nine clients have received master's degrees, 16 bachelor's degrees, and 25 associate's degrees—and 15 of their children have received college scholarships.[80]

These women, considered throwaways by society, transformed their lives and futures, along with the lives and futures of their children, through the CCM services provided to them. CCM helped them access each and every service, including funds for education and job training, to treat their condition of poverty. It became clear that CCM was making dreams come true. I didn't have research or outside evaluation ... yet. I did have proof, however, right before my eyes. Everyone has dreams, but for the first time the dreams of these women were met with realistic plans to make those dreams come true.

As our Matrix Partnership for Housing and Landlord Alliance program was evolving, we received a major donation from the Ladies of the Links Sorority organization: brand-new bedding. By now I had learned that beds without pillows and blankets constituted an incomplete donation. This generous sorority agreed. I personally negotiated the deals, maximizing our tax-free status, using my now-honed begging skills to garner freebies and extras as well.

We purchased beds and had them delivered for the moms and the kids, with all the bedding. Trucks pulled up from the suburban furniture store known from local commercials, yet rarely seen in these neighborhoods, to deliver and set up new beds with all the trimmings. With each delivery, mothers were crying, staff members were crying, and more than one said, "This is my first bed" (a statement their children will never have to make again). The Ladies of the Links, adopting the Matrix ladies, unequivocally demonstrated mentoring's power, not only with their donations but with real guidance in life skills, creating hope. Not just a handout, but a real hand up.

The power of mentoring and volunteerism

The women of the Links planted the seed, and I began to recognize their powerful impact on the homeless women in our program. These were strong, successful, African American women with a deep and abiding concern for Matrix's homeless women and their children. The effect was profound. To hear a client talking and commenting "Ms. Caliman said ...," the influence of the Links members was evident. The research, though limited, supports the power of such mentoring relationships.

There also is evidence that mentoring can have beneficial effects for both the mentees and the mentors who provide it. M. J. Karcher in "Cross-age Peer Mentoring" (2015) writes:

> Key outcomes on which changes have been reported in the mentoring literature are consistent with findings from adults-with-youths mentoring programs in schools. These include attitudes toward and connectedness to school and peers, self-efficacy, grades and academic achievement, and behavior problems, as well as games and conventional attitudes toward illicit and antisocial behavior.[81]

Mentoring at Matrix became part of the social fabric. Our clients began supporting other clients, their peers, in mentoring relationships. It wasn't assigned or mandatory; it just began happening as we organized more and more events for clients and their families, and they became the volunteers running the events. Although not documented due to funding limitations, many supportive relationships began occurring naturally during programming and events. Examples included women sharing rides, childcare, job openings, older kids helping younger kids with homework, teaching sports, and volunteering at our summer camps.

A culture of community support was developing. Although I had no analytics and still don't, the transformation I was witnessing was nothing short of breathtaking. In our shelter for homeless youths, the power of mentoring was palpable. Imagine the fear when a homeless, abused, or abandoned teen comes into a Detroit homeless shelter. It's scary. What few belongings these young people have must be screened, by strangers, clothes immediately washed (to reduce the incidence of lice and bedbugs), and temporarily replaced with shelter clothes.

Now the teen is in a "home" with other kids, each with his or her own set of troubles. Our staffers are kind, but it is the kindness of the other kids that is touching and brings the most security for the newbie coming in. It's a good feeling to hear one homeless teen say to another, "It's OK … you're safe here; the people who work here are nice, and you can eat anytime you want."

According to a study done by Big Brothers and Big Sisters, "students who meet regularly with their mentors are 52% less likely than their peers to skip a day of school and 37% less likely to skip a class."[82]

What I was witnessing was the evidence I needed. The research was just the frosting on my mentoring cake. Mentoring at Matrix became part of our social fabric. I'm not really sure where and when the mentoring and the volunteering began, but the benefits were plain as day. The research supported my common-sense observations.

Volunteers learn new skills, increase their socialization, are exposed to new and different people, have a positive impact on the community, enhance their sense of purpose (and achievement and accomplishment), explore new career options, improve existing ones, and develop and improve job skills. Volunteerism—giving of time, energy, and skill in support of another—is often more beneficial to the giver than the receiver.

First at Matrix, then later as a component of the developing standard of care, volunteerism has been integrated into protocols and is recognized as a vital aspect of treatment for the condition of poverty.

The research supported what we knew to be true after experiencing the benefits firsthand. According to 2005 and 1990 studies, "Those who give support through volunteering, experience greater health benefits than those who receive support through those activities."[83]

And a 2005 *Journal of Gerontology* report on altruism states:

The results of a survey of a large, ethnically diverse sample of older adults showed no association between receiving social support and improved health; however, the study did find those who gave social support to others had lower rates of mortality [than] those who did not, even when controlling for socio-economic status, education, marital status, age, gender and ethnicity.[84]

In a *U.S. News & World Report* article, Dr. Mark Snyder, a researcher from the Center for the Study of Individual and Society at the University of Minnesota, is quoted: "People who volunteer tend to have higher self-esteem, psychological well-being, and happiness." Accordingly, "All of these feelings increase as feelings of social connectedness increase."[85]

Research findings by Jane Piliavin and Hong-Wen Charng indicate that even at-risk teenagers who volunteer reap significant benefits. They cite a positive effect of volunteerism on grades, self-concept, and attitudes toward education, plus decreased drug use and large declines in dropout rates and teen pregnancies.[86]

Regardless of age, race, religion, or culture, people who volunteer do better socially, psychologically, physically, educationally, and economically. Yet, in those early years when I looked around Matrix, the volunteers looked like me.

We began setting the new expectations and creating a culture of volunteerism—infusing volunteerism into every program and at every opportunity. Our clients and their families became the Matrix volunteer army. The impact was very evident. For many of our clients, it was the first time outside of their family where they were the needed and not the needy. Their pride in helping us help others far exceeded our expectations. Clearly, there's a symbiotic quality in volunteerism.

A number of men got involved too: watching the parking lot, doing custodial tasks, helping in the classroom, supervising in the gym. At The Center (previously Mt. Zion church) space was offered at no cost to anyone who wanted to offer a free service to the community. The community-based volunteers started to teach sports, cheerleading, dancing, and exercise. Our gymnasium came alive.

Everyone has a dream

I watched with awe and gratitude as The Center and other programs were being transformed. Hope and help created the change. The culture was beginning to shift. By asking "What is your dream?" we began to actively "map dreams" for virtually all our clients. With CCM, hope was met with help to make many of those dreams a reality.

In 2015, my last year at Matrix, we booked 138,000 hours of volunteer service,[87] the bulk provided by our clients.

As our standard of care evolved, volunteerism was integrated into Map of My Dreams®, which is analogous to a treatment plan. In the process, clients would develop their future vision with their case manager. Volunteer work would then be used as a vocational pathway based on the career aspirations that clients identified in their personal Map of My Dreams.

Once defined, volunteerism was used as a vocational platform. For example, if the client dream was to be a teacher, the nearest Head Start program was the ideal volunteer platform; if she or he wanted to be a nurse, the closest clinic or hospital was contacted. Volunteer opportunities began changing lives and life trajectories.

The client was asked at intake "What is your dream?" *not* "What do you need?" Together the map would be defined, authenticating every service and support. The client was then in a partnership designed for his or her success. Working together, client and staff proved that poverty is not what defines a person—and the seeds of hope would be sown.

Volunteerism was integrated into the daily routine for women at the homeless shelter, for runaway youths in our juvenile-justice program, for seniors sewing for new mothers, for moms and dads helping at school. The act of helping others changed perspectives and attitudes. Although we had no measurements and no budget to document the volunteering, I knew the impact was deeply significant. No matter how old or young, what color or religion, the data we collected made it crystal-clear: Helping others changes who we are.

With the aid of 2-1-1, Matrix staff and volunteers could identify where to get needed services and together ensure not just information about programs but real access to all these programs by holding the network of service providers accountable. If CCM and a client were getting no response or poor treatment from an agency, the issue went up the management chain until dialogue between organizations occurred, right up to the CEO level. That's how it's done. That's how you take care of your customers. Behavior unchallenged is behavior unchanged.

My research continued.

Of predators and prey

I learned that a lack of understanding of predatory purchasing and lending practices infests the economics of being poor.[88] There is a strong correlation between financial literacy and the health and well-being of individuals, families, and communities, along with the vitality and efficiency of financial markets.[89]

Predatory lending practices are designed to take advantage of the less educated and the desperate, people unable to secure cash from any other source. By accepting high fees and/or high interest that grossly benefit the lender, the poor—often unaware, uneducated, or desperate—agree to such terms to their disadvantage.

Predatory practices include but are not limited to:

- Emphasizing the payment on interest only, creating lifelong, never-ending payments (not unlike the sharecropping system for many former slaves after the Civil War)
- Balloon loans
- Packing extras into loans, increasing the cost of insurance
- Excessive fees
- Excessive points
- Excessive interest due to bad credit
- Predatory loans characterized by high interest (pawn shops and payday lenders)

Payday loans have become a staple for many working-poor families in this country. The working poor, often unable to make ends meet between paychecks, go to a payday lender for an advance. Of course a fee is charged for the service. The next payday, with that much less money to work with, another advance is needed to purchase basic necessities. The payday loan becomes essential.

Each week, often with ever-increasing debt, pay is taken out of the pockets of the working poor. Payday lenders reap a fortune at the bottom of the financial-services pyramid. The payday-loan industry in the U.S. is valued at $46 billion annually,[90] built largely on the backs of the poor.

Due to poor credit, purchasers desperately in need of transportation to obtain and retain work frequently feel that they have no choice but to pay more than is reasonable for a car with high interest rates and penalties for late payment. These auto-sales lenders offer an auto-loan payment that focuses on interest payment, not principal. Lenders thereby create a treadmill effect, reaping a payment cycle that far outlives the value of the vehicle.

The practice of lenders deceptively convincing borrowers that interest-only minimum payments are affordable, not letting on that minimum payments never end, makes perpetual debt the indentured servitude of the 21st century. These businesses are making billions at the expense of the poorest and most in need.

In 2014 I was attending a Clinton Global Initiative (CGI) Conference in Denver, Colorado. My excitement was off the charts. The standard of care to treat poverty, now officially called Transition To Success® (TTS), had recently been recognized as a CGI initiative, and I was invited to present my work. I was assigned to the Financial Stability work group. During the conference I would spend hours with this group discussing issues related to financial stability. The room was filled with experts in lending and finance; I was way out of my league.

The conversations eventually turned into a lively discussion on the predatory-lending practices of pawn shops. The underlying message from this group was, "Why would anyone use a pawn shop for a short-term loan?" I attempted to explain the vital function of a pawn shop in a poor neighborhood's economy. Often the local pawn shop is the only path to food, groceries, medicines, or heat before the next check is in hand. People living in poverty rely on this service, one no bank would ever consider. The use of the pawn shop for short-term loans is in itself predatory lending. But predatory lending is usually the only option and preferred over no food or heat. Priorities change when you live in poverty, as does how you manage resources.

In poverty, Mother's gold bracelet may be a consistent source of short-term collateral, keeping the family above water from month to month. My perspective was dutifully and respectfully listened to, but my message was mostly lost. This audience, tasked to impact all strata of society, did not seem to understand the economics of the bottom of the pyramid.

Financial literacy

"Making the Case for Financial Literacy—2013" is a collection of statistics gathered from various sources by Jump$tart. This comprehensive resource makes it abundantly clear that financial literacy improves outcomes for children, teens, and adults. Teaching people, regardless of their age, how to manage money improves their financial health.[91]

Research supports the fact that low levels of financial literacy likely lead to poorer health, decreased quality of life, and lower education attainment levels.[92]

In order for financial literacy to be an essential component of people moving out of poverty, curricula must be designed specifically for the audience and focus on real-world examples. A curriculum of "Who's ripping me off and how?!" written at the third-grade level, taught in the neighborhood (preferably with additional supports of transportation and childcare), is what's needed. Meeting people where they are will help take them where they want to go.

To summarize: At Matrix we began implementing care management, volunteerism for children as young as 6, volunteering as a vocational pathway, peer mentoring, and financial literacy. Now, believe me, this was and continued to be done on a shoestring. There was no real plan or methodologies, and no funding was secured other than what was currently in place. We had no centralized client records—and no funds for data-collection systems or increased staffing at any level. We also had very few consistent analytics.

What we measured evolved over time. It included the tracking of immunizations, along with vision, dental, and hearing exams in Head Start; educational accomplishments for homeless women, runaway youths, and homeless youths; and our Youth Assistance Program for at-risk young people in the court-referred program. We started tracking senior rides to doctor appointments and meals served to all age groups. Our work began to take hold on multiple levels, and our results (still collected internally using paper and pencil) showed increasing promise.

Over the next five years, Matrix became transformed—first in appearance and presentation, then in atmosphere and culture. I believe that the transformation we were witnessing also was due to the culture of respect and hope those of us in leadership at Matrix were promoting organizationally, clinically, and fiscally. Included in our efforts were the integration of a customer focus, how we answered the phone, tracking call return times, making certain that voice mails didn't get full, and real advocacy for our customers—ensuring their access across the delivery system.

These developments at Matrix—including CCM support, mentoring, volunteerism, and financial literacy—led to what has become the Transition To Success model. TTS is the framework for understanding and treating the condition of poverty with uniform protocols and analytics that continually improved based on data driving practice.

For clients, all this created hope, and hope changes everything.

Chapter 10

How Does Transition To Success® Work?

Napkins are my canvas

I am a visual person. I like systems and processes written down. As I spent more time learning about the people and the Matrix programs, an internal system of care presented itself. Most often on napkins. I wish I would have saved those dozens of models I designed to represent how a client moved through the system of care. Across all programs we identified staff to be the care coordinators. We began doing in-services, teaching all Matrix programs about all other Matrix programs, creating cross-pollination. These were conditions we could control ... for the most part.

It was the macro system that was the tough nut to crack. There was no way Matrix or any organization could provide all the essential services needed to improve health and economic self-sufficiency. I realized that looking for funding to create a comprehensive delivery system at Matrix was simply not realistic. I needed a network.

Coming from healthcare, I knew all about networks. I built some of them. The provider network is the artery system delivering the healthcare services. The care is only as good as its network. In healthcare a diverse customer base needs and requires 24/7 access to complex, diverse, and specialized services to deal with the following: chronic conditions, medical emergencies, preventive care, specialties, outpatient, inpatient, aftercare, rehab, etc. All this requires extensive contracting to establish a comprehensive, full-continuum delivery system across rural, urban, suburban, and specialty populations.

That's what we needed—a network that unified health, human services, government, and education programs and services. We needed it ASAP, and we needed it for free. Necessity is the mother of invention.

We wanted—and our clients needed and deserved and had a right to—the $1.6 trillion funded delivery system already in place to help the poor in the United States.

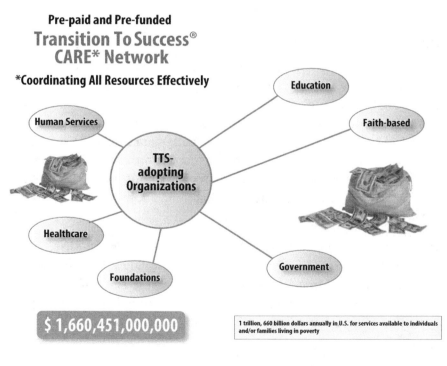

Pre-paid and Pre-funded
Transition To Success®
CARE* Network
*Coordinating All Resources Effectively

- Education
- Human Services
- Faith-based
- TTS-adopting Organizations
- Healthcare
- Foundations
- Government

$ 1,660,451,000,000

1 trillion, 660 billion dollars annually in U.S. for services available to individuals and/or families living in poverty

Source: Federal Office of Management and Budget, http://febp.newamerica.net/background-analysis/education-federal-budget

© 2016 Transition To Success®

We needed to organize, in the poorest and one of the most corrupt cities in the country, the disjointed system that was funded to care for and protect our clients. We began putting the network together. We identified providers by domain, health, human services, government, and education. We focused on integrating all essential, already-paid-for services that were necessary for helping people move out of poverty. Our new network would be funded by other people's money (OPM).

A delivery system in Detroit began to make itself known: a rich patchwork of programs and services, some more elusive than others, each patch with its own rules and regulations, some patches completely missing, partial patches, along with worn and tattered patches. This patchwork—the existing, funded delivery system, our OPM network of care—gradually revealed itself and became the TTS CARE (Coordinating All Resources Effectively) Network.

Follow the money

Our job, in the words of Tim Gunn (fashion consultant and TV personality—"Project Runway"), is to "Make it work" by maximizing every already-funded service outside of Matrix, at every turn for every client, and hold that system accountable. Follow the money.

We had to organize this complex, multi-domain system with no money and little technology. Who would have ever thought I would be lusting for the technology I so took for granted in healthcare? Phone books proved inefficient (seemingly always outdated). At that time, not so long ago, computers were not readily accessible at all our offices, much less in clients' homes.

Enter United Way of Southeast Michigan. The introduction of 2-1-1 in the Detroit Metropolitan Communities was a critical tipping point in the evolution of our system of care, Transition To Success (TTS). The 2-1-1 system was transformational, and our partnership was instantaneous. Although so many critics were complaining that "A phone number by itself has little impact," 2-1-1 provided instant backbone for the TTS standard of care.

The 2-1-1 technology became the framework for our care managers, caseworkers, direct-care workers, parent advocates, et al.—and for our clients to enable us to identify every viable resource in the community. This technology provided the information on the *who, what, where, when,* and *how.* Asking "What is your dream?" became the standard question, and the Map of My Dreams became each client's treatment plan, confronting both poverty itself and the delivery system—better allowing the latter to actually deliver on its promises.

Of course, 2-1-1 critics were in fact correct in some measure: Information alone for a client in poverty is often futile. This was confirmed by my experience as a secret shopper. Without unlimited phone minutes, ability to read, transportation, funds to get from here to there at different times ... with different requirements and paperwork, accessing information and services was close to impossible.

At Matrix the client works together with his or her TTS-trained staff person to shape a client's dream, not just develop a plan to meet his or her immediate needs. Together they create the plan, use 2-1-1 to map the path, and demand access to the services. All the while the client is learning how to self-advocate and feel what it's like to be a customer, not a beggar.

Hope

Those early days in a corrupt, blighted Detroit, with poverty everywhere and an overwhelming sense of learned hopelessness for both clients and the staff working with them ... The hardest question to answer was: How do you bring hope back? This I couldn't find in the research, but then the path revealed itself. We realized that when we asked "What is your dream?" ... in the client's eyes a glimmer of light and hope began to shine. It became a staple question, and we found everyone has dreams, no matter the age. The difference is that for so many living in poverty no one has worked with them on the steps needed to achieve those dreams.

This simple question has changed the playing field. It shifts the relationship from giver/receiver to planner and customer. Asking about the dream brings much-needed hope to the equation. Hope has not yet been demonstrated as a best practice, but without a doubt hope is a game changer. Our job in TTS is to make dreams come true—and respond to immediate needs. By recognizing dreams and providing the map to achieve them, the dreams become tangible—no longer just pie in the sky. We have asked hundreds if not thousands of people (all ages, all races, all religions): "What is your dream?" We learned that everyone has a dream.

In the poorest city in the country, even during the roughest of economic times, the housing crisis, the collapse of the auto industry, the bankruptcy of the city, and the emergency management of Head Start and Detroit Public Schools, the dreams were rich, especially for the young people. Hope was a free yet essential commodity. Thank God, because without money and with a fractured delivery system, sometimes hope was all we could afford.

When a young person in Detroit is asked "What is your dream?" the response is often "I want to be a professional basketball player." Statistically speaking, of course, it's a long shot—as most skeptical adults are all too quick to point out. In fact, the common response from just about everyone, old and young alike, is "What are the chances?"

Living in poverty makes the dream even more of a fantasy. Maybe we should map to a more realistic dream, like gym teacher? Kids' dreams may seem unattainable, especially to well-meaning adults— or adults who are themselves feeling hopeless. It may seem reasonable to redirect. But I knew different. Not from the research … I knew it in my heart.

As a woman, as a mother, sometimes hopelessly optimistic and grandiose in my own dreams, I know that our job, our responsibility, is to bring hope and help to this often dark, sad, heartbreaking city. We are not buzz kills. Hell, yes, we map to basketball player. That's what we do.

So, young man, with so much promise: "How do you get to be a professional basketball player?" He knows ... just ask, inquire. You have to go to school, be healthy, get on a team, practice, and yes ... get decent grades and go to college. This is possible. I'll say it again: We aren't buzz kills. Dreams are for the making.

Map your dream

The old adage goes: "Give a man a fish and he eats for a day; teach him to fish and he eats for a lifetime." This reframing from "need" to "dream" costs nothing, but it can have a transforming effect. Working with clients to create their Map of My Dreams, analogous to the treatment plan in healthcare, is essential to first understanding the problem, identifying resources and services, ensuring access to those services, providing support, and tracking results.

Ah, now the tough part: making dreams come true. This is real life, and making dreams come true can be extremely challenging. Let's face facts: Not every dream does come true—at least not on the first try or in the way you might expect.

If at first you don't succeed, well, try, try again.

When describing the system of care, I am often asked, "So, what do you do when clients relapse?" OK. Let's think about this. When patients' cancer returns, what do we do? We get them treatment. The sooner the better. What if those patients still are smoking and the cancer returns, what do we do? There is no debate. We get them treatment—for the cancer and the nicotine addiction. We do our best to get them what they need.

Here's the double standard. Drug and alcohol addiction is a medical condition, with clinical guidelines, diagnostic codes, and billable services. No longer just a weakness: "Strong evidence suggests that both disorders are, at least in part, influenced by genetic factors."[93]

So why then do we limit care to addicts, discontinue their benefits, and allow the sickest and neediest among us to live like animals on the streets of our cities? I know I'm not alone when my heart aches at seeing a homeless person on the street, especially in the dead of winter.

The plight of the homeless in Detroit was never more glaring to me than at our Experience Matrix event. Staff wanted to conduct a breakfast event under a tent in one of our parking lots to save money, even knowing it might be chilly. We moved ahead. More than 175 donors came to our breakfast. We had makeshift lighting, and a dozen client volunteers ushered them to their seats. The lights were bright, the tables were set, and the stage's sound system was ready.

Our guests, expecting a party, were greeted warmly, but the Michigan air was cold, bone-chilling cold. As it turned out, they were the huddled masses, wearing caps and gloves as they ate.

The message, though completely unintended, crystalized and was reinforced by the powerful messages from client volunteers who emotionally described what this audience was merely tasting. Experience Matrix indeed became an "experience." That morning, in a small way, nearly 200 people felt what it's like to be cold, just one small aspect of homelessness. Experience Matrix was a taste of life without a home.

I remember this event vividly because of my feet. I wore lady business shoes with nylon hose to this event. I arrived at 6 a.m. and left around 10 a.m. Just four hours outside—in a tent wearing a coat and gloves. By mid-morning my feet were burning in pain from the cold, and my heart sank at the realization that people with addictions and mental illness, abandoned, were living just blocks away from the event.

Pouring salt into a wound

In poverty the incidence of addiction and mental illness is significantly higher. Denying treatment for an illness often caused by poverty and induced by environmental exposures is pouring salt into an already-open wound. This is the character-flaw mentality at the foundation of much of our nation's response to addiction, mental illness, and poverty: "There is something wrong with you; you are poor, you are weak, you have no self-control, and we are done taking care of you."

In poverty, relapse is often punished by extraction from the program funded to care for those needing help the most. In the TTS culture, on the other hand, addiction, mental illness, and poverty are met with integration of available treatments, supports, and resources to address addiction and poverty. In poverty, treating addiction requires a response to the social determinants of health. Poverty and addiction are often co-occurring disorders; both require treatment. Failure to address one without the other is putting a bandage on a broken arm.

So the short answer to the question, "What do you do when clients (often addicts) relapse?" It's simple; we get them treatment using whatever OPM (other people's money) is available. When people are sick, relapse happens.

Get them treatment. Easier said than done. TTS is designed, at every level of the organization, to hold the delivery system accountable. This system of accountability breeds respect for the customer and is essential in eroding the character-flaw mentality prevalent across most of the delivery system: "If paid professionals are going to help me make calls and demand services I am eligible for—and are willing to take my case up the chain—I must be important." This action of accountability reinforces hope and empowers the client, the direct-care professional, and the management team, because all are making a difference. Accountability provides the backbone and the realization that the dream is possible. Poverty is treatable.

It is the dead of winter in Detroit. The local shelter, well-funded by numerous organizations, is the OPM key to our delivery system. A Matrix client living in temporary shelter with her children shares with her care manager worker that there is no heat at the shelter, and there hasn't been in quite some time. The client is afraid to complain for fear she will lose her precious spot, and she and her children will be on the street.

The worker contacts the shelter staff without revealing the client's name. Yes the heat is out, it has been out, and staff doesn't know what the plan is. No worries, though. In the interim, families have each been given a small electric space heater.

So the worker, with client observing, takes the issue up the shelter chain, asking questions, sharing concerns, and noting there is no real plan. Matrix management, hitting a dead end, is trained to take it up to the next level, the vice president of Clinical. Once the case is reviewed, the VP calls the CEO at the shelter, advises about the situation, and documents our attempts and lack of results.

The CEO had been unaware. The heat was repaired within 24 hours of the call to the CEO. Behavior unchallenged is behavior unchanged.

In poverty, that challenge—demanding real service—is essential not just for the client, but equally if not more important for the direct-care worker, the provider organizations, and the institutions all generating billions of dollars to care for the poor.

Transition To Success evolved into a process

Hope. Asking not, "What do you need?" Asking, "What is your dream?"

Help. To immediately address basic needs of food and shelter— maximizing and accessing every available service for food, clothing, shelter, healthcare.

Map your dream. Identify every support step and program, then develop a plan to make the dream a reality. This starts with immediate unskilled employment; everyone needs to learn to work, and volunteerism becomes a vocational platform. If your dream is being a teacher, volunteer at the Head Start closest to your home. If your dream is to be a nurse, volunteer at the closest clinic or hospital. If your dream is to be a hair stylist, volunteer at a salon. As noted in Chapter 9, volunteerism is for many the first time being the needed, not the needy. The experience is transformational. As clients volunteer, entry-level jobs usually follow.

Mapping dreams creates real pathways to enrollment in literacy or English as a second language. Find a peer mentor, someone in your community a little farther ahead, working his or her way out; together you are both stronger. Concrete examples include financial literacy,

GED, skilled employment training, and eventually a living wage—always working, always giving back, always looking forward. Yes, making dreams come true.

OPM

So who pays for 2-1-1 services at United Way of Southeast Michigan? OPM. Who pays for the shelter? OPM. Who pays for literacy? OPM. Who pays for energy assistance? OPM. We didn't need to know who funded all the services.

But we did need knowledge of and access to all those services: food, shelter, housing, identification, healthcare, treatment for substance-abuse and mental-health issues, heat assistance, workforce, literacy, financial literacy, GED, community-college loans, stipends, childcare, transportation … all became part of the Transition To Success CARE Network. CARE, our acronym—Coordinating All Resources Effectively—paid for by our generous sponsors, OPM.

In the words of Denise, once homeless, now with a master's degree: "I didn't have to worry about food, housing, none of those things. They took care of all of them so I could go to school and study."

By maximizing existing, paid-for positions in existing programs, TTS became a methodology, not a program. Train existing staff; don't create new programs. TTS was integrated into existing programs and processes. An organizational culture shift occurred. The client is the customer. No wrong door.

The customer is greeted by staff members trained in understanding poverty as a treatable condition. They understand their job, their role in changing—and sometimes saving—lives.

The clients/customers meet their TTS-trained direct-care worker and are asked, "What is your dream?" Together client and professional:

- Complete self-screening, using the Arizona/Minnesota
  Self-Sufficiency Assessment Domains (see Appendix);
  this tool was initially developed in Maricopa, Arizona

- Review scores and triage all urgent and emergent areas (suicidal, homicidal, child/adult protection issues)

- Contact 2-1-1 to identify and provide specific information for all eligible community resources services and supports for client/family across health, human services, education, and government, as well as any gaps to be overcome to help the dream come true

- Organize resources by priority/eligibility to actualize dream(s) to include volunteerism, financial literacy, and opportunities for mentoring

- Explore and engage any faith-based support systems—and discuss gaps and potential gap strategies

- Begin accessing the CARE Network, learning preparedness, assertiveness, and follow-through in the process

Chapter 11

Vision Without Backbone
Is Merely Hallucination

Seeing is believing

The integration of hope changed everything. It wasn't based on any research or statistics. This is what I saw, regardless of demographics. I knew it to be true for the clients and then, to my surprise, also for our staff and for the organization. I'm not sure when it happened or how it happened, but at some point I realized that's what we were doing.

Although our paper-and-pencil stats were promising, creating more fodder for fund raising, I knew what I needed. I began to yearn for real research and evaluation. My begging (I mean searching) for funding ensued. Long story short … In 2008 we convinced The Community Foundation of Southeastern Michigan to give us a chance. The foundation's challenge to us, however, turned out to be daunting indeed.

The CFSM directive was clear: Apply Transition To Success to 150 returning citizens (men and women leaving prison) headed for the Osborn neighborhood in Detroit. Really? This population was coming to the poorest city in the nation, before the Affordable Care Act was passed by the U.S. Congress in 2010, and to one of the most violent Detroit neighborhoods. This was the TTS test.

It was no secret. The reentry population faces many of the most difficult challenges with regard to economic self-sufficiency. The literature documenting not only the struggles but also the sheer numbers of incarcerated individuals and returning citizens in the U.S., including the disproportionate number of people of color, specifically African American males, is far-reaching and immense in volume. *The Wall Street Journal* reports that in the United States 2.3 million persons are incarcerated at a cost of $80 billion annually.[94]

Our challenge? To play a key role in helping returning citizens have improved health and economic self-sufficiency using existing community resources—this during dark times in Detroit's history, with the vast majority of clients uninsured. Across Detroit—and most evident in the Osborn neighborhood—were high poverty, high crime, high unemployment, the effects of the Great Recession, the collapse of the auto and housing industries, widespread corruption at City Hall, and impending city bankruptcy. At the time it certainly looked like the perfect storm for our work to fail.

We accepted the challenge. Working with our partners, our job was to help transform the lives of these 150 individuals, maximizing existing, already-funded programs with care management, volunteerism, mentoring, and financial literacy. This was our first documented effort in building a network of care.

I remember the excitement of this development, the first research grant under my tenure. The Michigan Department of Corrections, a grant partner, gave us the addresses of the entire returning-citizen population in the Osborn neighborhood. I drafted a lovely letter, attentive to the need for third-grade readability. We mailed hundreds of letters, with a Matrix logo, not the corrections logo. Our goal: to serve the first 150 clients in our new program called "Welcome Home, Osborn."

We received fewer than 10 calls. Our letters had little impact for a population that either could not read or did not use letters as a primary means of communication. Failure comes in all shapes and sizes. But if at first you don't succeed ...

Our next approach: a picture postcard. The pictures depicted a person in prison, a person being released from prison, making a call to the number indicated, and then going to work. This did the trick! During our three-year study we ended up serving more than 200 returning citizens, and our results, though not statistically significant due to sample size, changed everything.

More than five times less recidivism

After three years the recidivism rate back to prison, in this statistically insignificant study, was 7%![95] To put that percentage in perspective, a 2011 study by the PEW Charitable Trusts Center indicated that more than 40% of former inmates usually return to prison within three years.[96]

In 2013 the cost for Michigan prisons was $93.65 per day or $34,183 per year per prisoner. The cost for Transition To Success at Matrix was $4.17 per day—or $1,523 per year per client.

The return on investment for every returning citizen not re-incarcerated was $89.48 per day or $32,660 per client per year. This does not include the economic benefits as a productive member of society.

Our results confirmed reality. No one wants to be poor or break laws in order to survive. No one wants to go to prison or return to it. No one wants their children to grow up with one or both parents behind bars—or without heat or a good school, a safe neighborhood, and decent clothes. No one wants to be poor. The human spirit, the way we are wired, drives us to survive, the best we can, even in a nation where the have-nots are too often victimized by the very system charged with providing a safety net for them.

This first TTS study (with the roughest population, in the poorest city, during tough economic times) created the foundation for transformational change to begin. The concept for a standard of care—uniform protocols and analytics to treat the condition of poverty, an environmentally based medical condition—was born.

I Can See Clearly Now!

Pitching a vision

Our first piece of research was a small study by any measure. The results, as previously stated, were not statistically significant. But for us, the results of the "Welcome Home, Osborn" study were profound. Both quantitatively and qualitatively, we were part of and witnessed lives transformed.

Although not funded for follow-up with the 200-plus clients, the Welcome Home, Osborn pilot cleared the path for important next steps because now we had so much more than just anecdotal Matrix stories. We had data, which reflected results with the roughest population in the toughest of times. Data and a relationship (see next paragraph) just may have changed the course of "poverty history." I guess time will tell.

A colleague, previously the CEO at a Detroit not for profit, was hired as a program officer at the Kellogg Foundation. I met with Dan Varner for lunch in Detroit and described how our data defined our success. I pitched the vision: uniform protocols and analytics to treat poverty, using the same model as an environmentally induced medical condition. The lunch meeting lasted about 90 minutes. Mr. Varner liked the idea. He suggested I write up the proposal and submit it to Kellogg. I did.

That luncheon, seemingly no different from hundreds of other meetings with many good people, was a dynamic tipping point in the development of a standard of care to treat poverty. Months later, after writes and rewrites, budgets and multiple drafts, the Transition To Success grant proposal to the Kellogg Foundation was submitted in 2011—and approved in 2012. A new paradigm, treating poverty as a medical condition, was born.

We thus began the work of creating the standard for children, teens, adults, and seniors, along with the analytics to measure the impact related to myriad social determinants. In partnership with Detroit's Marygrove College, the curricula and analytics (the ability to measure outcomes related to social determinants) were developed.

Our new baby, a paradigm shift with supporting curricula to train individuals in the methodology, was becoming a reality. Integrating care management, volunteerism, financial literacy, and peer mentoring into programming required a template or how-to manual. Just as we wanted clients to make their Transition To Success with a defined plan, we now had the opportunity to develop the first instrument to teach the industry the recipe for treating the condition of poverty and measuring the results.

Like most recipes or how-to books, however, the first recipe is just the beginning. The development of the first curricula and analytics to treat poverty as a medical condition was never intended to be a final product. As with virtually all other industries and endeavors, the attempt was and remains the integration of continuous quality improvement. This first iteration of curricula teaching how to treat poverty will forever be a Model T. Just as healthcare, the auto industry, and manufacturing are always improving, so now, with the integration of CQI, is the practice of the treatment of poverty. Research and data must drive practice.

I knew that without CQI, Transition To Success was nothing more than another great idea. Nonetheless, my spirits were not dampened. I had seen the transformation of lives and an organization. Hope became a stimulant to everything I did. My determination and focus to have a new paradigm for understanding poverty—and TTS as a national standard of care—had begun.

Building a plane while flying it

Build it, and they will come. We were flying a plane while building it—out of tin cans, mind you: writing grants, training organizations to train other organizations, implementing, and all measuring the same analytics. TTS was now:

- Scalable, with curricula
- Sustainable, using OPM
- Measurable, using the nationally accepted Arizona/ Minnesota Self-Sufficiency tool
- Multi-generational, with a pathway for seniors, adults, teens, and children as young as 5
- A social enterprise where lead organizations in a community generate unrestricted revenue by training across their community
- Transformational, with each community gaining momentum as more organizations across the domains adopt the protocols

A standard of care requires scalability, the ability to reach and engage large audiences. Our audience is massive: the delivery systems for healthcare, human services, government, education, and faith-based programs. TTS scalability is achieved with the development of curricula—recipe books, if you will—that teach trainers how to train direct-care workers in understanding and integrating the best practices of care management, financial literacy, mentoring, and volunteerism into their operations for children, teens, adults, and older adults. New curricula can be developed for special populations (foster care, juvenile justice, homeless, vets, tribal communities). Most recently a curriculum was developed for children, coaches, and parents engaged in organized soccer in Colorado.

As part of the curricula, those getting trained also develop knowledge and understanding of OPM. Other people's money is key to treatment, and practitioners learn how to identify, maximize, and hold accountable the funded delivery system in their community. They are trained to integrate federal, state, county, city, and faith-based programs and opportunities that align with the client's goals. This type of accountability can only be accomplished in an organizational culture that supports the direct-care worker. Management's support and advocacy up to and including the CEO are the key ingredients to empower staff serving clients on the front lines. When CEOs hold each other accountable, the messaging to staff and client is crystal-clear: Our customers matter.

Holding a delivery system accountable requires measurable, meaningful outcomes. Like so many things in TTS, this too is in its infancy. The Arizona/Minnesota Self-Sufficiency tool provides a simple, easily integrated tool that can offer measurable insights for both practitioner and client into current status, emergent and urgent priorities, areas of stability, and progress toward goals. Data collected from agencies using this tool can be aggregated to support understanding of what is and isn't working—and how we can improve, including the way we collect and measure data.

Outcomes data generated by the Arizona/Minnesota Self-Sufficiency tool can then be a pathway to increased revenues from grant funding. Unrestricted revenues can be generated when TTS is integrated as a social enterprise. The adopting TTS organizations, with trained trainers, lead the training of TTS across their communities. This social-enterprise model is community-based and community-led, and it creates a rich environment for pollination, adoption, and expansion of the standard of care across many providers in a community.

I became obsessed (I mean convinced). I felt increasingly confident that this work would have a significant impact on the understanding and treatment of poverty in this country. Who wouldn't want continually improving, consistent protocols and analytics to treat the condition of poverty? A system where research and data drive practice, not just good intentions. The liberals, the conservatives, the rich, the poor. It makes sense clinically, fiscally, morally.

For this work to transform understanding and treatment, to become a true standard of care, it must be accepted across the industries of healthcare, human services, government, education, and faith-based entities. And it must be continually improved upon. Research and data drive practice. I realized poverty shares a commonality with other environmentally based medical conditions. This environmental-exposure frame of understanding—comparing the condition of poverty, for example, to lead poisoning and mesothelioma (cancer caused by exposure to asbestos)—helped to crystallize the new paradigm. Regardless of age, race, religion, or culture, when individuals are exposed to poverty, statistically speaking, they will be sicker, less productive, more costly, and die younger than their counterparts.

Understanding poverty through the lens of being a treatable condition across healthcare, human-services, education, government, and faith-based audiences addresses and debunks the character-flaw mentality. As noted in Chapter 7, understanding poverty as an environmentally based treatable condition stops the blame/shame game because poverty is not about who you are, it's about where you live and the conditions you are exposed to.

No matter who they are, when people must constantly deal with food insecurity, racism, inadequate housing, poorly performing schools, high crime rates, and lack of access to living-wage jobs, transportation, and healthcare, they will not only be less healthy but also have earlier mortality.

Environmental conditions constitute a major cause of poverty and directly impact health. The literature identifies the following exposures as social determinants of health:

- Lack of access to healthful food, safe places, healthcare services, and stable housing

- Environmental pollution

- Lower educational levels, including a lack of basic health literacy
- Cumulative stress and trauma

The World Health Organization defines social determinants of health as "the conditions in which people are born, grow, live, work, and age. The circumstances are set by the distribution of money, power, and resources at global, national, and local levels."[97]

Economically distressed communities, particularly communities of color in the United States, have the poorest access to such essential services as grocery stores, medical care, and transportation. And they have the fewest social supports to overcome or eliminate these obstacles.

The connection between health and environment is irrefutable. A recent analysis of the medical records of hundreds of thousands of Americans found that—regardless of what they eat, how active they are, and other personal factors—residents of low-income neighborhoods usually die sooner than people living in wealthier communities.[98]

The new paradigm

The evolution of poverty from a social condition, an enigma too large to conquer due to weakness and alleged character flaws, to poverty as a health condition began. I would contend that poverty is primarily caused by:

- Environmental exposures, not by weakness, laziness, unhealthy values, color of skin, religion, or dishonesty; environmental exposures include lack of access to basic needs of food, clothing, shelter, transportation, living-wage employment, and healthcare
- An unequal education system that promotes a caste system of haves and have-nots across healthcare, education, and employment. Just like a caste system, poverty tends to induce shame in that it both oppresses and humiliates

Environmental exposures also are identified by Philip E. DeVol in *Getting Ahead in a Just-Gettin'-By World* in his research continuum on four causes of poverty: individual behaviors and circumstances, community conditions, exploitation, and political/economic structures.[99]

Understanding poverty's causes and the inextricable links between health and environment are how we build a standard of care—not by simply proclaiming, "I have the cure!" Rather, we must embrace constructive feedback, the research and data, to lead us to the next, new and improved level of treatment. Industries have benefited from years of continuous quality improvement; CQI, which is embedded in the culture of this country, must now be integrated into the treatment of poverty.

With Transition To Success we become the pioneers—for the first time treating poverty with uniform protocols, analytics, and CQI. We become the pioneers and trailblazers, and I know there's gold in "them thar hills." Our hope, our dream, our mission must be that the work we do today eventually becomes "old school"—the sooner the better. I can see clearly; this movement is only getting started.

Let's take a closer look at TTS.

Yes, But Does It Work?

You want me to do what?

Here's one way of articulating the TTS mission statement:

By training an organization's direct-care workers to coordinate care across multiple delivery systems, by training administrators to support their direct-care workers to hold the community-based, already-paid-for system accountable, and by training everyone across the organization that poverty is not a character flaw but a treatable condition—and ensuring that clients, just like funders, are customers to be valued and respected—*outcomes for clients improve* as does the culture of the organization and community as a whole.

I know this to be true from experience; years of Matrix paper-and-pencil outcomes tell the story.

In 2014–15 at Matrix Human Services:

- "Eighty-one and a half percent of students participating in individualized care management TTS programming demonstrated at least one grade-level improvement in reading and math."

- "Of the 210 participants enrolled in the Matrix Employment Center, 45% were placed in jobs, training programs, or internships while enrolled in the program.

This happened despite the 14.6% unemployment rate in Detroit. This does not include job placements after exiting the program."

- "Seventy-six clients who were enrolled in the Matrix appointment center without a GED obtained their GED during their time with the program."

- "In a 90-day follow-up survey, 78% of youths in the Matrix runaway shelter remained enrolled in school or a training program; 93% reported having medical insurance; and 98% reported having access to healthcare."

- "Ninety days post-discharge: 14% of runaway youths maintained employment, 14% continue to actively look and 72% remained in school or higher education."

- "In the Matrix programming for young people at risk of delinquency, 89% of participants reduced school truancy, 90% reduced substance abuse, 92% reduced incorrigible behavior, 90% increased their grade-point average, and 85% increased their life-skills and conflict-management abilities."[100]

These are just some of the outcomes accomplished at Matrix during fiscal year 2014–15 with Transition To Success integrated across programs. These outcomes across all programs are not research-based, they're not from an independent evaluator, and they're not statistically significant. Yet these paper-and-pencil records told us, unequivocally, that people of all ages want to do better. But most just don't know how. These outcomes also tell us clearly that poverty is not a character flaw; poverty is a treatable condition.

Of bread, butter, and manna from heaven

OK. This is good. But the bread and butter, the whole enchilada, is independent evaluation. This I knew—and it was our Achilles heel.

Timing is everything. Head Start in Detroit collapsed. At first this development might have seemed problematic, but ultimately it was manna from heaven. I credit Dave Bing, former mayor of Detroit (2009–13) and Hall of Fame NBA basketball player (mostly with the Detroit Pistons), who I believe recognized a department gone bad, suffering a fatal condition and resistant to the strongest of antibiotics. It simply wasn't amenable to change. The feds moved in, and Detroit Head Start went under emergency management. Almost immediately, there was renewed hope for young children and their families in Detroit. But would it be the gift of life—or the kiss of death—for Matrix?

The federal government's emergency management team was in place for two years. During that time our administrative-overhead rate was severely reduced, and the city went bankrupt. This clogged our cash flow yet again through no fault of our own. The banking industry's lack of faith in Matrix intensified in a city where the multi-million-dollar Head Start business was going out to bid. These were the roughest fiscal times in my career; I was once again dreading payroll Fridays.

In addition to the fiscal stranglehold, the competition inside and outside the city was fierce. Survival of the fittest. If Matrix lost this bid, our 30-year-old Head Start program would close. Without Head Start, the fiscal backbone of the organization, Matrix would have to close its doors—400 employees without work. Without Head Start, Matrix would be no more. Everyone across the organization knew about this possible fate. It was do or die. I expected a mass exodus of employees understandably in need of secure employment; it didn't happen.

Our yearlong preparation for the "Matrix Head Start: the Next Generation" proposal to the federal government began. I had no resources to pay consultants or have special data reports or gap analysis completed. Maximizing OPM, we utilized resources made available to us by the local foundations and our Matrix team of subject-matter experts. I transferred the director of Head Start to a one-year temporary assignment—in order to work directly with me and our grant writer to develop a Head Start proposal that maximized all that Head Start has to offer children.

Our simple, research-based premise was that the best way to improve health and educational outcomes for children is to improve the health and economic self-sufficiency of their parents. Matrix Head Start: the Next Generation was born—integrating existing, TTS-funded positions and training dollars.

Our program provided comprehensive services through comprehensive care management across an entire delivery system: health, human services, government, and education. Our program also integrated independent research and evaluation of the impact of treating poverty with a new paradigm—uniform protocols and measurements.

Further, our program was completely redesigned to encompass comprehensive services across the areas of health, human services, government, and education for pregnant mothers, as well as infants and children from birth to age 5.

We waited on edge for almost a year, anxiously wondering if our Matrix way of life would be preserved, if our legacy would continue, if our system of care would finally have the research and evaluation essential to establish a standard of care.

The news finally came. Matrix was awarded the largest expansion of Head Start in Detroit's history! Matrix was now the biggest federal demonstration project in the city. When we received the call, we knew the future was ours, the responsibility enormous, and the funding very substantial for the agency and community. The grant: more than $200 million in funding over the next five years—and a fully funded Transition To Success research project. This was unreal—*and* real.

Shortly after our Head Start award, TTS-related data continued to tell the story. In 2015 independent evaluation results at Matrix in Head Start and at Family Service of Detroit and Wayne County (an outpatient mental-health program) were realized. All services provided in our study were within existing funding streams. Research and evaluation comprised the only additional funding secured.

TTS Independent Evaluation Results

Matrix Head Start: SSM* Domains with a Significant Change in Mean Scores, Winter 2014 to Spring 2015

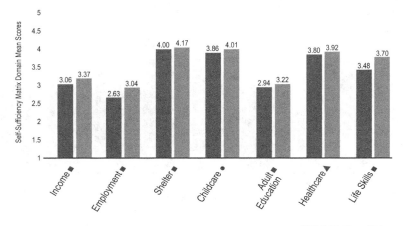

• Indicates a statistically significant change (p<.05) in means from pretest to posttest
▲ Indicates a statistically significant change (p<.05) in means from pretest to posttest
■ Indicates a statistically significant change (p<.001) from pretest to posttest

*SSM: Self-Sufficiency Matrix

Matrix Head Start: SSM Domains with a Significant Change in Mean Scores, Winter 2014 to Spring 2015

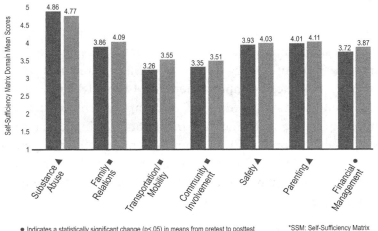

• Indicates a statistically significant change (p<.05) in means from pretest to posttest
▲ Indicates a statistically significant change (p<.05) in means from pretest to posttest
■ Indicates a statistically significant change (p<.001) from pretest to posttest

*SSM: Self-Sufficiency Matrix

Source: Transition To Success® Final Evaluation Report, 8/29/2015, W. K. Kellogg Foundation, Grant: P3018954

TTS Independent Evaluation Results (continued)

FSDWC*: SSM Domains with a Significant Change in Mean
Scores from Pretest (January 2013 through February 2014)
to Posttest (November 2013 through April 2014)

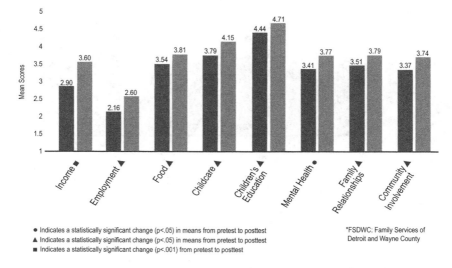

● Indicates a statistically significant change (p<.05) in means from pretest to posttest
▲ Indicates a statistically significant change (p<.05) in means from pretest to posttest
■ Indicates a statistically significant change (p<.001) from pretest to posttest

*FSDWC: Family Services of
Detroit and Wayne County

Source: Transition To Success® Final Evaluation Report, 8/29/2015, W. K. Kellogg
Foundation, Grant: P3018954

Results in the first two charts indicate that in the Matrix Head
Start program (which included TTS integration, using the Arizona/
Minnesota Self-Sufficiency tool) Head Start parents experienced
statistically significant improvement in 14 of 18 domains. This
included but was not limited to income, employment, education, and
healthcare. Of note is the increase in parents' willingness to report a
substance-abuse concern in the home when interviewed again after
one year. In a culture of treatable conditions, it is likely that the fear
and stigma associated with addressing substance abuse are minimized
and replaced with trust and hope.

The third slide represents results of a Detroit outpatient behavioral
health clinic (personnel trained in TTS), with an average length of
stay of six outpatient visits in a Medicaid managed-care system. The
results, as reported by research and evaluation partner Evaluation

Strategies, indicate statistically significant improvement in eight of 18 domains. Areas of improvement included income, employment, and mental health. Addressing poverty and responding to the social determinants of health with children and adults living in poverty, particularly important in a Medicaid plan, is key to effectively responding to mental and physical conditions.

These statistically significant results reinforced my emerging path. It was time to leave Matrix and pursue a national standard of care to treat poverty. This had become my calling.

Today Matrix continues to lead the largest expansion of Head Start in Detroit's history with a five-year project bringing $200 million-plus into the Detroit economy. Matrix was now positioned to demonstrate that indeed the best way to improve the health and educational outcomes for children is to improve the health and economic self-sufficiency of their parents.

The Transition To Success framework for understanding and treating poverty was confirmed in the 2015 Kids Count in Michigan Data Book (child well-being in Michigan, its counties, and Detroit): "For children to thrive, their parents must have access to postsecondary education and training; affordable, high-quality childcare; and family-supporting jobs."[101]

Chapter 14

The Next Generation

A standard of care to treat poverty

Sometimes in life there comes a time when something deeply significant is happening. I never expected it, but it happened. At some point—I'm not really sure when or how—I realized that applying a standard of care with uniform protocols, analytics, and clinical pathways has profound impact on those in need. I also realized that a standard of care to treat poverty could have a transformational effect on society and its belief systems.

A standard of care is actually feasible. Transition To Success does not require millions of dollars or controversial legislative changes. TTS is affordable and accessible today—for individuals, organizations, and communities.

I knew this work needed to go far beyond the walls of Matrix. Running a large, complex organization, with more than 100 funding streams and serving thousands every week, was a huge responsibility deserving full-time attention. My focus needed to be on a sustainable, scalable, social-enterprise model for Transition To Success. This was the only way to achieve far-reaching, collective impact: Maximizing existing resources, coordinating care, volunteerism, financial literacy, peer mentoring, and defined analytics were all part of the protocols.

Now what was needed was a business model to encourage other organizations to adopt Transition To Success, which was not about creating little Matrixes everywhere or trying to expand our operational footprint outside Detroit. Scalable transformational change through community-based initiatives could not be perceived as competition on any level. Not for profits need to generate unrestricted cash.

Giving other not for profits and individual practitioners the opportunity to make money—in our industry called social enterprise—is all the rage. Transition To Success Train the Trainer did just that. Transition To Success-trained trainers, for a fee, train new TTS trainers at new TTS-adopting organizations. The first-adopting agency in a community becomes the training resource, for a fee, leading what is to become a community-based initiative.

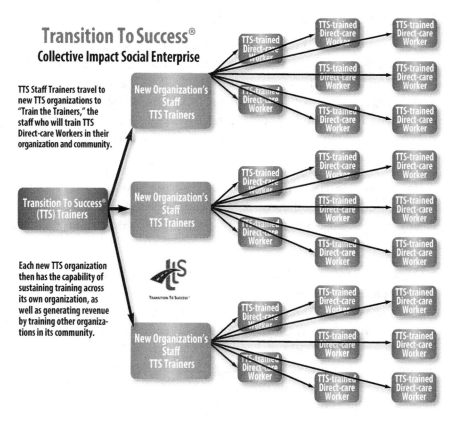

© 2016 Transition To Success®

Now training other organizations, such agencies together create a Transition To Success CARE Network, utilizing uniform protocols and analytics. With the Train the Trainer model, TTS became a scalable, sustainable, measurable, multi-generational social enterprise driving collective impact and transformational change.

TTS trainers train the next generation of TTS trainers at the adopting, community-based organization. These TTS trainers then lead the TTS training, implementation, and data collection across their community.

It works. By early 2016 TTS had pilots in several programs and cities across the country. Eight hundred professionals were now trained in TTS.

It is happening—most notably in Memphis, Tennessee. The Assisi Foundation of Memphis, Inc. has been leading the most comprehensive TTS CARE Network in the nation, building on its "Bridges Out of Poverty" initiative. More and more organizations have been joining the network, eventually with support from the mayor of Memphis and the United Way of the Mid-South. Once funders lead, the swarm mentality often follows. Follow the money.

As of this writing, our final piece of the puzzle—the ability to collect and analyze multi-site TTS data in a system that also integrates industry research to continually improve the standard of care to treat poverty—has been realized: the next generation, the new frontier, to go where no one has gone before … true integration of CQI across the delivery system, continually evolving the treatment of poverty. TTS, in my view, is more than a great idea; it is becoming a reality and a force.

Let's review ...

Understanding and Treating the Condition of Poverty

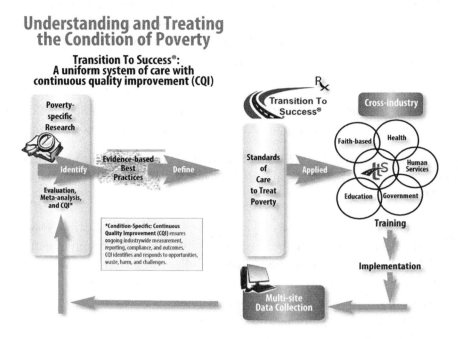

© 2016 Transition To Success®

This flow chart illustrates, in a practical way, how to understand and treat the condition of poverty with Transition To Success. To the far left please note the research on poverty and health, education, government, foster care, the homeless (the list goes on). Industry leaders review that research. As an industry leader, I have identified in my review four best practices: care management, volunteerism, financial literacy, and mentoring.

Thanks to the Kellogg Foundation, we had the first curricula developed to train trainers and workers in how to integrate these practices and, thanks to United Way and the Arizona/Minnesota Self-Sufficiency Assessment, we can measure impact on the social determinants of health. Today, with new curricula, these standards with uniform protocols and prescribed analytics are being distributed and implemented across the country in projects large and small. TTS training and implementation create an opportunity for multi-site TTS data collection that is then integrated with research, evaluation, and meta-analysis, driving the CQI process to continually redefine and refine the ability to treat poverty.

This work at some point must inevitably become outdated and replaced with better ways of treating poverty. We know there are better ways. Then those too must be replaced with even better ways. TTS is today a Model T. It's great for its time, a game changer, but like the Model T, the models must improve with time. Who would have imagined that today some cars can drive themselves? This is what happens when research and data, yes, *drive* practice.

This essential component—collection and analysis of multi-site data—is a critical next frontier. That frontier is upon us. Civic Health, now a TTS partner, has invested in and has developed technology that integrates TTS into care-management systems, electronic medical records, claims systems, chronic-disease management, even eligibility determinations. Screening for social determinants in medical settings, education, human services, and government programs can now be accomplished quickly and inexpensively.

Recently a national research institute and not for profit, Michigan Public Health Institute (MPHI), under the leadership of Dr. Renee Canady, took the next critical step. MPHI has taken the risk, making the investment of its resources to secure the funding needed to build the technology to complete the standard-of-care feedback loop. A true standard of care is now within reach. Finally, poverty will be treated with both research and data driving practice, not just good intentions.

MPHI is positioned to lead the development of new and improved curricula based on the research and data. MPHI also is being positioned to lead a system of care to treat the condition of poverty.

A standard of care to treat the condition of poverty can never be left in the hands of a single individual. The standard must outlive the originator or face extinction. Nor should it be in the hands of an entity driven largely by profit. TTS must be carefully placed in the arms of an organization whose mission and vision are aligned with the treatment and elimination of poverty—and with a commitment to health equity.

I believe MPHI is that organization.

What Legacy Will We Leave?

Taking action in the face of fear

For the first time since I was 14 years old, I am without a steady paycheck as I write this book. Bills exceed income, and I have only a few weeks to generate more income at the newly established TTS, LLC. I am afraid. Of course, I've been afraid before. I cling to the knowledge that bravery is not the absence of fear. Bravery is the ability to take action in the face of fear, including the fear of failure.

I embrace the words of Robert F. Kennedy, U.S. Attorney General and Senator:

"Only those who dare to fail greatly can achieve greatly."

Even if I fail and eventually have to seek out a "real" job, I know, without a doubt, this is what I must do. Even my family agrees.

My new husband has been working his federal job by day and offering TTS administrative support at night. My daughter, a family law attorney while on maternity leave, was negotiating TTS contracts. I write this book, not knowing precisely what the future holds, but knowing that exciting things are in store.

My original plan of working with Matrix in a consultant role and continuing to lead the CQI component of its research was not to be. New leadership often brings new vision. My next challenge is to complete the system and be a catalyst for seeking to transform poverty in the United States. The vision requires extensive investment in information technology to collect and integrate data and analytics from multiple TTS sites across multiple industries. MPHI has accepted the challenge.

Building on that challenge, a national standard of care requires that TTS-adopting organizations form across the country, become TTS Centers of Excellence, and have their data collected and analyzed by MPHI. TTS-adopting organizations across human services, healthcare, government, education, and even faith-based entities will pay a nominal fee to have their data analyzed and integrated with other TTS organizations and the best research of the day to continually improve practice. Organizations then become accredited and individual practitioners certified.

This system of care becomes an industry that goes beyond good intentions—as evidenced by our outcomes, lives saved, futures made, money saved by government, and an expensive, extensive, siloed delivery system transformed.

The problem is poverty, not the poor

Most importantly, this work is intended to promote a national understanding of what it is to be poor, sick, hungry, and in need ... an understanding that who we are is reflected by how we treat each other, particularly the most vulnerable among us. We need a societal acceptance that the problem is hunger, not the hungry, and housing, not the homeless. Indeed, the problem is poverty, not the poor who struggle to navigate one of the most complex, dysfunctional, ineffective delivery systems in the industrialized world.

This work must promote a response to poverty based on science, data, and treatment protocols, finally laying ignorance and intolerance to rest, where they belong, in the dustbin of American history.

> "Every man's burden is our burden. Where poverty exists, all are poorer. Where hate flourishes, all are corrupted. Where injustice reigns, all are unequal."
>
> –Whitney M. Young Jr., U.S. Civil-Rights Leader

Chapter 16

Call to Action

"Nothing happens unless first we dream."

—Carl Sandberg, U.S. Poet

'What is your dream?'

This is the foundation of Transition To Success. TTS was built on the belief that the human spirit can overcome, that anything is possible, especially in America. Ask anyone, "What is your dream?" and you give the gift of immediate affirmation that you believe in them, in their spirit, and in their capability of achieving anything. Asking "What is your dream?" in and of itself inspires hope. Hope is the special sauce, the rocket fuel, the not-so-secret ingredient that can change everything. But dreaming and hoping alone don't change reality.

As noted, vision without backbone is merely hallucination. Inspiring others to dream is the easy part. To be effective, it must be followed by support, advocacy, and accessible pathways to overcome the plethora of obstacles required to improve health and economic self-sufficiency. If a dream is to learn to read, the mere existence of a literacy program across town is only a single component of a complex problem. A real path must ensure that the TTS client can actually get to the program, a program offered at times that don't interfere with employment at a non-living-wage job. In addition, childcare has to be coordinated and, by the way, do you need food (because it's hard to learn to read if you're hungry)?

Each individual path is unique, based upon dream, age, circumstance, and community. Each dream requires support and advocacy, always teaching how to self-advocate and self-navigate the disparate systems of care as a customer, not a beggar. Each dream has a defined path for giving back, using volunteerism as a vocational platform and a source of pride, accomplishment, and importance. Hope with a backbone.

All of us have dreams, regardless of our circumstances. I have a dream to transform the paradigm for understanding poverty in this country from character flaw to treatable condition, to ensure the integration of clinical pathways across delivery systems, to measure our success or lack thereof, and to use that information to continually improve our work. Sometimes my dream feels like a long, never-ending drama with big highs (presenting at Harvard) and gut-wrenching disappointments (sometimes being turned away by foundations).

A growing army of believers

With the support and advice of what has become hundreds of others interested in the work, a growing army of believers understands that in the U.S. 70 million people on Medicaid, 48 million of them living in poverty, don't want to be poor. All are hoping—and many are praying for a better life.

> "People want to get better; they just don't know how."
>
> —Denise McNair[102]

Our new job is to convince a nation to change, to accept that poverty is not a weakness, a character flaw, or a choice. We also want people to understand that some aspects of poverty are the direct result of exposure to toxins and must be accepted and treated as a medical condition. This paradigm shift, this culture change, is essential. Only then will policy, programming, and a lasting future of tolerance emerge—along with thousands if not millions of people making their own personal Transition To Success.

Changing the world view is not enough, however. My dream calls for healthcare, human-services, government, education, and faith-based entities to adopt uniform protocols and analytics to treat the condition of poverty, then report their outcomes to a single source for analysis in order to refine clinical pathways and measure the return on investment, also known as ROI.

How much money will we be saving by actually treating the condition? What will happen to rates of incarceration, mental illness, substance abuse, foster care, and complex medical conditions if we treat poverty itself? What is the ROI? It has to make sense from all angles, not just the human angle. No money, no mission. That is the world we live in.

But even that isn't enough. My dream becomes the dream of many, inspiring the dreams of many, many more: tangible, affordable, collective impact leading to transformational change for millions and their offspring for generations to come.

The work will not be done until this vision is reality in our land of freedom, justice, and opportunity.

"I alone cannot change the world, but I can cast a stone across the waters to create many ripples."

–Mother Teresa, Roman Catholic Nun of India:
Nobel Peace Prize Winner, 1979, and
Saint Teresa of Calcutta, 2016

A national movement

This book is one of those stones. This book is not just a story of epiphanies and revelations in my life or the cultural transformation of an organization. The purpose of this book is to transform the understanding of and response to poverty in the United States of America. This book is an instrument of mass communication designed to engage and build a national following in a national movement.

The movement is already happening. Other professionals are presenting TTS in large and small settings across the country. In 2015 I was invited by Ruby Payne to present at a national poverty conference; Dr. Payne is the woman who has so greatly influenced my thinking along this journey. At the conference, a colleague was presenting a workshop on TTS. Walking into that workshop almost took my breath away. As Mother Teresa said, ripples from a stone.

In 2103 I presented TTS at a small conference in Washington, D.C. Maria, an attendee from Memphis, is director of a small program for children and families living with HIV/AIDS. Maria went back to Memphis and spoke to her CEO, who subsequently spoke to Dr. Jan Young, executive director of the Assisi Foundation of Memphis, Inc. Believing in the model, Dr. Young incentivized a diverse group of providers to take the training and collect the data; the mayor of Memphis endorsed our project, then came an endorsement from the director of the Memphis United Way.

These developments led to my introduction to Dr. Payne. She recognized the power of Bridges Out of Poverty and Transition To Success united. Dr. Payne then created for me the opportunity to write and publish this book.

> "The test we must set for ourselves is not to
> march alone but to march in such a way that
> others will wish to follow us."
>
> –Hubert Humphrey, U.S. Vice President and Senator

This is how social change happens, through the pollination of many seeds. Someone learns about TTS, connects someone else, who knows someone else. This is how I got to Harvard, The Aspen Institute, and to foundations. These accomplishments all occurred because someone else believed. This is how TTS became part of the Clinton Global Initiative. The power and influence of individuals with a shared vision become the engine of change for multitudes.

"When spider webs unite, they can tie up a lion."

—African Proverb

Poverty is the lion; we are the spiders.

"Never doubt that a small group of thoughtful, committed people can change the world. Indeed, it is the only thing that ever has."

—Margaret Mead, U.S. Anthropologist

We are the small group of thoughtful, committed people, each of us contributing as we can.

Call to Action, Phase 1: A word not spoken is a message never heard

This is your call to action. If you are taking the time to read this book, you know what's going on. Now step beyond watching and become part of this revolution. If you were arrested on a charge of helping others, would there be enough evidence for a conviction? You may ask, "What can I do? I am only one. I don't have money or influence."

In its simplest form, your call to action is intolerance of intolerance. When you see it, hear it, or experience it, let your voice regarding what is right be heard. Whether it be a racist joke at a party, bullying, or an off-the-cuff statement about "those people," be silent no more. Behavior unchallenged is behavior unchanged. As noted, when you see intolerance, be intolerant. This call to action usually costs us little, but together we are a strong voice. Raindrops unite and create a storm; eventually they can create floods of change.

When society, which is composed of individuals, turns a blind eye to social injustice, crimes against humanity occur. Sadly, examples abound in our nation's history: the enslavement of a race of people for 250 years, the near genocide of this land's original indigenous inhabitants, and discrimination to this day against people of color in particular.

Even today we realize our world and country haven't changed very much as we witness numerous closed doors to tens of thousands of men, women, and children fleeing their homes due to unrelenting violence and religious extremism, only to find many borders barricaded, barbed-wire fences, and refugee camps. Closer to home, the necessity of a Black Lives Matter movement is a sad commentary on this nation's culture of intolerance.

Hatred and intolerance must be confronted—directly and with one's voice. United, our collective voice becomes a call for social justice. Let your voice be heard, and let your actions support others. Volunteer. You will be richer for it. This you can do.

Are you ready, willing, or able to take the next step?

Call to Action, Phase 2: Get behind the wheel

If you want to take the next step, this is your opportunity to be a driver of social change. Who do you know, what can they do, and how can we connect? Begin engaging others. Become part of the movement. Speak to the paradigm shift of poverty as a treatable condition. Use social media. Use this book, Facebook, the TTS website, your own website, a blog.

If you are part of an organization working with the poor (or know someone working at an organization that works with the poor), be the voice to bring TTS to that organization. Make it happen; make the connection. You are the power of one.

> "The potential for greatness lives within each of us."
> —Wilma Rudolph, U.S. Olympic Gold Medalist

This is your call to action. Don't just read the book, talk about it, recommend it to others, volunteer, lead social change in your world.

> "You must be the change you wish to see in the world."
> —Mahatma Gandhi, Indian Activist

If you are in a position of wealth and/or influence, look for opportunities to make a difference in your community and country.

> "Huge fortunes that flow in large part from society
> should in large part be returned to society."
>
> –Andrew Carnegie, U.S. Industrialist and Philanthropist

Small fortunes work too. Get involved; get in touch. Invest your money in long-lasting social change. Even a small business can lead community-based social change. We can show you how. Sponsor a community forum or, better yet, sponsor a [your company name here] TTS CARE Network. Business and corporate leaders, along with other influential citizens, can ask their community to come together and involve other leaders in a community-engagement strategy. Social change doesn't happen by accident.

Yes, you can attack poverty in your own community, in your corner of the world. If just one leader steps up, each community can begin its own implementation, and each community can begin to understand what services are really working and where the gaps are. Each community can have a campaign at the beginning of the school year to "Make Dreams Come True," with kids mapping their dreams and planning how to make them come true.

Further, each community can transform its culture from despair and shame to hope and confidence. This is now being done in small pockets around the country, and the movement is growing. Be a part of the change. You can make a difference; together we can change lives and futures.

> "From those to whom much is given, much is expected."
>
> –Bill Gates, Microsoft Founder and U.S. Philanthropist
> (paraphrasing Luke 12:48b in New Testament of Bible)

Call to Action, Phase 3: Together we can do this

"Lead me, follow me, or get out the hell out of my way."

–George S. Patton Jr., U.S. General in World War II

If you are a funder, a policymaker, a program officer at a foundation, or a corporate executive in government, education, healthcare, or human services, you are in a position directly connected to potential collective impact. Your power and influence are essential components of sustainable, scalable, and transformational social change.

Funders are invited to unite to require funded organizations to treat the condition of poverty; they also can then follow clinical protocols and collect and report uniform analytics to demonstrate effectiveness. Their collective data from multiple sites is then analyzed in relation to the most up-to-date research, thereby driving improved clinical protocols.

Continuous quality improvement defines new protocols to treat poverty that are continually integrated across the delivery system. This becomes a system of care that treats poverty with research and data driving practice, not just good intentions. When funders require uniform protocols, the provider industries can be expected to acquiesce and adopt standards.

In Detroit within miles of one another, I can name five multi-service, multi-million-dollar, human-services organizations. These organizations serve tens of thousands of people collectively, overlap clients, overlap services, compete for donors, and compete for grants. Each of the human-services organizations, working hard with good intentions, provides care in its own microcosm.

With regard to the treatment of poverty, the same is true in healthcare, education, and government programs. It is now feasible for our fractured system to be unified clinically and operationally with the integration of uniform treatment protocols and analytics. It doesn't require an act of God, Congress, or a bazillion dollars. It does require engagement and support from individuals and organizations at all levels across the spectrum of society.

To anyone and everyone reading these words, if you want to respond to this call to action (or if you have questions), we want to hear from you. What are you thinking and doing and how can we help you? Please visit: www.TransitionToSuccess.org

This book has been designed to change—incrementally or substantially—the way you understand and respond to poverty. I hope I have been successful. More importantly, I hope I have inspired you to become part of the movement.

Together we can do this.

Appendix

Transition To Success®
19 Self-Sufficiency Assessment Domains

Transition To Success®
19 Self-Sufficiency Assessment Domains

DOMAIN	1 – In Crisis	2 – Vulnerable
1. Shelter/Housing	Homeless or threatened with eviction	In transitional, temporary, or substandard housing; and/or current rent/mortgage payment is unaffordable (over 30% of income)
2. Employment	No job	Temporary, part-time, or seasonal; inadequate pay, no benefits
3. Income	No income	Inadequate income and/or impulsive or inappropriate spending
4. Food and Nutrition	No food or means to prepare it; relies to significant degree on other sources of free or low-cost food	Household receives federal SNAP (Supplemental Nutrition Assistance Program) benefits
5. Childcare	Needs childcare, but none is available/accessible and/or child is not eligible	Childcare is unreliable or unaffordable; inadequate supervision is problem for childcare that is available
6. Children's Education	One or more school-age children not enrolled in school	One or more school-age children enrolled in school, but not attending classes
7. Adult Education	Literacy problems and/or no high school diploma/GED are serious barriers to employment	Enrolled in literacy and/or GED program and/or has sufficient command of English to where language is no barrier to employment
8. Medical Coverage	No medical coverage with immediate need	No medical coverage and/or great difficulty accessing medical care when needed; client may be in poor health

Source: Adapted from Arizona/Minnesota Self-Sufficiency Domains[103]

3 – Safe	4 – Building Capacity	5 – Empowered
In stable housing that is safe but only marginally adequate	Household is in safe, adequate, subsidized housing	Household is safe, adequate; unsubsidized housing
Employed full time; inadequate pay; few or no benefits	Employed full time with adequate pay and benefits	Maintains permanent employment with adequate income and benefits
Can meet basic needs with subsidy; appropriate spending	Can meet basic needs and manage debt without assistance	Income is sufficient, well-managed; has discretionary income and is able to save
Can meet basic food needs, but requires occasional assistance	Can meet basic food needs without assistance	Can choose to purchase any food that household desires (makes healthy choices)
Affordable, subsidized childcare is available but limited	Reliable, affordable childcare is available; no need for subsidies	Able to select quality childcare of choice
Enrolled in school, but one or more children only occasionally attending classes	Enrolled in school and attending classes most of time	All school-age children enrolled and attending on regular basis
Has high school diploma/ GED	Needs additional education to improve employment and/or to resolve literacy problems to be able to function effectively in society	Has completed education/training needed to become employable; no literacy problems
On publicly provided health plan	Can get medical care when needed but may strain budget	Is covered by affordable, adequate health insurance

(continued on next page)

Transition To Success®
19 Self-Sufficiency Assessment Domains (continued)

DOMAIN	1 – In Crisis	2 – Vulnerable
9. Life Skills	Unable to meet basic needs, such as hygiene, food, activities of daily living	Can meet a few but not all needs of daily living without assistance
10. Family Relations/ Support Network	Lack of necessary support from family or friends; abuse (domestic violence, child) is present or there is child neglect	Family/friends may be supportive but lack ability or resources to help; family members do not relate well with one another; potential for abuse or neglect
11. Transportation and Mobility	No access to transportation, public or private; may have vehicle that is inoperable	Transportation available but unreliable, unpredictable, unaffordable; may have vehicle but no insurance, license, etc.
12. Community Involvement	Not applicable due to crisis situation; in "survival" mode	Socially isolated and/or few social skills and/or lacks motivation to become involved
13. Parenting Skills	Safety concerns regarding parenting skills	Parenting skills minimal
14. Legal	Current outstanding tickets or warrants	Current charges/trial pending; noncompliance with probation/parole
15. Mental Health	Danger to self or others; recurring suicidal ideation; experiencing severe difficulty in day-to-day life due to psychological problems	Recurrent symptoms that may affect behavior but not danger to self/others; persistent problems with functioning due to mental health symptoms

Source: Adapted from Arizona/Minnesota Self-Sufficiency Domains

3 – Safe	4 – Building Capacity	5 – Empowered
Can meet most but not all daily living needs without assistance	Able to meet all basic needs of daily living without assistance	Able to provide beyond basic needs of daily living for self, family, and others
Some support from family/friends; family members acknowledge and seek to change negative behaviors; are learning to communicate and support	Strong support from family or friends; household members support each other's efforts	Has healthy/expanding support network; household is stable, and communication is consistently open
Transportation available and reliable but limited and/or inconvenient; drivers are licensed and minimally insured	Transportation generally accessible to meet basic travel needs	Transportation readily available and affordable; vehicle adequately insured
Lacks knowledge of ways to become involved	Some involvement (advisory group, support group) but has barriers, e.g., childcare, transportation	Actively involved in community
Parenting skills apparent but not adequate	Parenting skills adequate	Parenting skills well-developed
Fully compliant with probation/parole terms	Successfully completed probation/parole within past 12 months; no new charges filed	No active criminal-justice involvement in more than 12 months and/or no felony criminal history
Mild symptoms may be present but are transient; only moderate difficulty in functioning due to mental health problems	Minimal symptoms that are expected responses to life stressors; only slight impairment in functioning	Symptoms absent or rare; good or superior functioning in wide range of activities; no more than everyday problems or concerns

(continued on next page)

Transition To Success®
19 Self-Sufficiency Assessment Domains (continued)

DOMAIN	1 – In Crisis	2 – Vulnerable
16. Substance Abuse	Meets criteria for severe abuse/dependence; resulting problems so severe that institutional living or hospitalization may be necessary	Meets criteria for dependence; preoccupation with use and/or obtaining drugs/alcohol; withdrawal or withdrawal avoidance behaviors evident; use results are in avoidance or neglect of essential life activities
17. Safety	Home or residence is not safe; immediate level of lethality is extremely high; possible Child Protective Services involvement	Safety threatened; temporary protection available; level of lethality is high
18. Disabilities	In crisis – acute or chronic symptoms affecting housing, employment, social interactions, etc.	Vulnerable – sometimes or periodically has acute or chronic symptoms affecting housing, employment, social interactions, etc.
19. Financial Management (Added by TTS)	Bankruptcies, foreclosures, evictions	Outstanding judgments, garnishments

Source: Adapted from Arizona/Minnesota Self-Sufficiency Domains

3 – Safe	4 – Building Capacity	5 – Empowered
Use within last six months; evidence of persistent and recurrent social, occupational, emotional, or physical problems related to use (disruptive behavior or housing problems); problems have persisted for at least one month	Has used during last six months but no evidence of persistent or recurrent social, occupational, emotional, or physical problems related to use; no evidence of recurrent dangerous use	No drug use/alcohol abuse in last six months
Current level of safety minimally adequate; ongoing safety planning essential	Environment safe; however, future of such uncertain; safety planning important	Environment apparently safe and stable
Safe – rarely has acute or chronic symptoms affecting housing, employment, social interactions, etc.	Building capacity – asymptomatic – condition controlled by services or medication	Thriving; no identified disability
Aware of credit score, needs Credit Repair Plan	Moderate budgeting skills, has bank account but no savings plan	Manageable budget and ability to save; bank account

Endnotes

[1] Leonard, 2015

[2] U.S. Census Bureau, 2016

[3] Crain's Detroit Business, 2013

[4] Annie E. Casey Foundation, 2016; Kennedy, 2015

[5] Annie E. Casey Foundation, 2012

[6] Abbey-Lambertz, 2014

[7] Data Driven Detroit, 2012

[8] "Detroit's Shocking 47 Percent Illiteracy Rate," 2011

[9] Kallenbach & Smitherman, 2012

[10] Center for American Progress, 2015

[11] Michigan League for Public Policy, 2016

[12] Michigan's Campaign to End Homelessness, n.d.

[13] United Ways of Michigan, 2014

[14] Annie E. Casey Foundation, 2013

[15] Children's Defense Fund, 2016; Kids Count Data Center, 2016a

[16] Adamson, 2012

[17] Shaefer & Edin, 2014; U.S. Census Bureau, 2016

[18] Ingraham, 2014

[19] Corak, 2006

[20] MacDorman et al., 2014; Kiersz & LoGiurato, 2015; BBC News, n.d.

[21] Addy, Engelhardt, & Skinner, 2013a

[22] Addy, Engelhardt, & Skinner, 2013b

[23] Addy, Engelhardt, & Skinner, 2013a

[24] Coley & Baker, 2013

[25] Jiang, Ekono, & Skinner, 2016

[26] Ianzito, 2015

[27] Castillo, 2013

[28] Coley & Baker, 2013

[29] U.S. Office of Management and Budget, 2013

[30] Kania & Kramer, 2011

[31] Jolin, Schmitz, & Seldon, n.d.

[32] Holcomb, 2016

[33] California Newsreel, 2008

[34] National Center for Charitable Statistics, n.d.

[35] Kids Count Data Center, 2016b
[36] Swanson, 2015
[37] Patterson, 1995
[38] Koppelman & Goodhart, 2008
[39] Lee, 2014
[40] Stuber & Kronebusch, 2004; Stuber & Schlesinger, 2006
[41] Donovan, 2015
[42] Ibid.
[43] Clay, 2015
[44] Payne, 2013
[45] Nolen, 2015
[46] Fincham & Cain, 1986; Peterson, Maier, & Seligman, 1993
[47] Koppelman & Goodhart, 2008
[48] Komisar, 1977
[49] Godfrey & Wolf, 2016
[50] Swanson, 2015
[51] Surowiecki, 2014
[52] Fagan, 2014
[53] Lathrop, 2014
[54] Desilver, 2015
[55] Addy, Engelhardt, & Skinner, 2013b
[56] Elliot, Song, & Nam, 2013
[57] Davis et al., 2016
[58] Child Trends Databank, 2015
[59] Kallenbach & Smitherman, 2012
[60] Robbins, Stagman, & Smith, 2012
[61] Ianzito, 2015
[62] Swanson, 2015
[63] Muennig et al., 2010
[64] Ali, 2013
[65] Children's HealthWatch, 2011
[66] Coley & Baker, 2013
[67] *Professional Guide to Diseases,* 2012
[68] "Abraham Maslow Quotes," 2016
[69] Radawski, 1999
[70] Flier, 2016
[71] Joint Commission on Accreditation of Healthcare Organizations, 1994
[72] World Health Organization, 2016
[73] Robert Wood Johnson Foundation, 2011
[74] Council on Community Pediatrics, 2016
[75] Braverman & Gottlieb, 2014; Commission on Social Determinants of Health, 2008
[76] Jemal et al., 2008
[77] Freedman et al., 2000
[78] Woltman et al., 2012

[79] Matrix Human Services, 2016

[80] Ibid.

[81] Karcher, 2015

[82] Big Brothers Big Sisters of America, 2016

[83] Corporation for National and Community Service, 2007; Piliavin & Charng, 1990; Post, 2005

[84] Brown, Consedine, & Magai, 2005

[85] Moeller, 2012; Clary, Snyder, & Stukas, 1996

[86] Piliavin, J. A., & Charng, H. W., 1990

[87] Matrix Human Services FY 2014/2015 outcomes; more information available upon request from www.matrixhumanservices.org

[88] Federal Deposit Insurance Corporation, Office of Inspector General, 2006

[89] Harnisch, 2010

[90] Yahoo Finance, Mandi Woodruff, 2015

[91] Jump$tart, 2013

[92] Lyons, 2007

[93] Dick & Arpana, 2008

[94] Holcomb, 2016

[95] Kahle Research Solutions, 2012

[96] Schwartz, 2014

[97] World Health Organization, 2016

[98] Wessler, 2009

[99] DeVol, 2013, p. 42

[100] Matrix Human Services, 2016

[101] Michigan League for Public Policy, 2015

[102] Matrix Human Services, 2013

[103] Minnesota Housing Finance Agency, n.d.

References

Abbey-Lambertz, K. (2014, May 16). Detroit's infant mortality rate is double the national average, but here's what they're doing to help mothers. *The Huffington Post.* Retrieved from http://www. huffingtonpost.com/2014/05/16/detroit-preterm-births-make-your-date_n_5339160.html.

Abraham Maslow quotes. (2016). AZQuotes. Retrieved from http://www.azquotes.com/author/9574-Abraham_Maslow

Adamson, P. (2012). Measuring child poverty: New league tables of child poverty in the world's richest countries. Innocenti Report Card 10. Retrieved from https://www.unicef-irc.org/publications/pdf/rc10_eng.pdf

Addy, S., Engelhardt, W., & Skinner, C. (2013a). Basic facts about low-income children: Children under 6 years, 2011. National Center for Children in Poverty. Retrieved from http://www.nccp.org/publications/pdf/text_1076.pdf

Addy, S., Engelhardt, W., & Skinner, C. (2013b). Basic facts about low-income children: Children under 18 years, 2011. National Center for Children in Poverty. Retrieved from http://www.nccp.org/publications/pdf/text_1074.pdf

Ali, S. S. (2013). A brief review of risk-factors for growth and developmental delay among preschool children in developing countries. *Advanced Biomedical Research, 2,* 91. doi:10.4103/2277-9175.122523

Annie E. Casey Foundation. (2012). Data snapshot on high-poverty communities. Retrieved from http://www.aecf.org/resources/data-snapshot-on-high-poverty-communities/

Annie E. Casey Foundation. (2013). The 2013 kids count data book. Retrieved from http://www.aecf.org/resources/the-2013-kids-count-data-book/

Annie E. Casey Foundation. (2016). Detroit: Background information. Kids Count in Michigan Data Profile 2016. Retrieved from http://www.mlpp.org/wp-content/uploads/2016/03/dbprofiles2016detroit.pdf

BBC News. (n.d.). World prison populations. Retrieved from http://news.bbc.co.uk/2/shared/spl/hi/uk/06/prisons/html/nn2page1.stm

Big Brothers Big Sisters of America. (2016). Big impact—proven results. Retrieved from http://www.bbbs.org/site/c.9iILI3NGKhK6F/b.5961035/k.A153/Big_impact8212proven_results.htm

Braveman, P., & Gottlieb, L. (2014). The social determinants of health: It's time to consider the causes of the causes. *Public Health Reports, 129* (Supplement 2), 19–31. Retrieved from http://www.ncbi.nlm.nih.gov/pmc/articles/PMC3863696/

Brown, W. M., Considine, N. S., & Magai, C. (2005). Altruism relates to health in an ethnically diverse sample of older adults. *Journal of Gerontology, Series B, Psychological Services and Social Sciences, 60*(3), 143–152.

California Newsreel. (2008). Unnatural causes: In sickness and in wealth [Transcript]. Retrieved from http://www.unnaturalcauses.org/assets/uploads/file/UC_Transcript_1.pdf

Castillo, M. (2013, October 28). Children who grow up poor shown to have smaller brain volume. *CBS News.* Retrieved from http://www.cbsnews.com/news/children-who-grow-up-poor-shown-to-have-smaller-brain-volume/

Center for American Progress. (2015). Talk poverty: Michigan 2015. Retrieved from https://talkpoverty.org/state-year-report/michigan-2015-report/

Child Trends Databank. (2015, December). Teen homicide, suicide, and firearm deaths. Retrieved from http://www.childtrends.org/wp-content/uploads/2014/10/70_Homicide_Suicide_Firearms.pdf

Children's Defense Fund. (2016). Each day in America. Retrieved from http://www.childrensdefense.org/library/each-day-in-america.html

Children's HealthWatch. (2011, June). Federal programs that protect young children's health. Policy Action Brief. Retrieved from http://www.childrenshealthwatch.org/upload/resource/fedprogs_brief_jun11.pdf

Clary, E. G., Snyder, M., & Stukas, A. A. (1996). Volunteers' motivations: Findings from a national survey. *Nonprofit and Voluntary Sector Quarterly.* doi: 10.1177/0899764096254006

Clay, R. A. (2015). Fighting poverty. *Monitor on Psychology, 46*(7), 77. Retrieved from http://www.apa.org/monitor/2015/07-08/cover-poverty.aspx

Coley, R. J., & Baker, B. (2013, July). Poverty and education: Finding the way forward. Educational Testing Service. Retrieved from https://www.ets.org/s/research/pdf/poverty_and_education_report.pdf

Commission on Social Determinants of Health. (2008). Closing the gap in a generation: Health equity through action on the social determinants of health. World Health Organization. Retrieved from http://www.who.int/social_determinants/final_report/csdh_finalreport_2008.pdf

Corak, M. (2006). Do poor children become poor adults? Lessons from a cross country comparison of generational earnings mobility. IZA Discussion Paper No 1993. Retrieved from http://ftp.iza.org/dp1993.pdf

Corporation for National and Community Service. (2007, April). The health benefits of volunteering: A review of recent research. Retrieved from http://www.nationalservice.gov/pdf/07_0506_hbr.pdf

Council on Community Pediatrics. (2016). Poverty and child health in the United States. Pediatrics, 137(4). doi:10.1542/peds.2016-0339

Crain's Detroit Business. (2013). 2013 giving guide. Retrieved from http://www.crainsdetroit.com/assets/PDF/CD91615111.PDF

Data Driven Detroit. (2012). State of the Detroit child. Retrieved from https://datadrivendetroit.org/files/SGN/D3_2012_SDCReport_Updated.pdf

Davis, M. M., Kolb, C., Reynolds, L., Rothstein, E., & Sikkema, K. (2016, March 21). Final report of Flint Water Advisory Task Force. Retrieved from https://www.michigan.gov/documents/snyder/FWATF_FINAL_REPORT_21March2016_517805_7.pdf

Desilver, Drew. (2015, July 23). 5 facts about the minimum wage. Pew Research Center. Retrieved from http://www.pewresearch.org/fact-tank/2015/07/23/5-facts-about-the-minimum-wage/

Detroit's 'shocking' 47 percent illiteracy rate. (2011, May 6). The Week. Retrieved from http://theweek.com/articles/484910/detroits-shocking-47-percent-illiteracy-rate

DeVol, P. E. (2013). *Getting ahead in a just-gettin'-by world: Building your resources for a better life* (Rev. ed.). Highlands, TX: aha! Process.

Dick, D. M., & Arpana, A. (2008). The genetics of alcohol and other drug dependence. *Alcohol Research and Health, 31*(2), 111–118. Retrieved from http://pubs.niaaa.nih.gov/publications/arh312/111-118.pdf

Donovan, D. (2015, December 13). The housing trap. *The Baltimore Sun Sunday.* Retrieved from http://www.pressreader.com/usa/baltimore-sun-sunday/20151213/281487865293751

Elliot, W., Song, H-a., & Nam, I. (2013, March). Relationships between college savings and enrollment, graduation, and student loan debt. *Research Brief No. 13-09.* Center for Social Development. Retrieved from https://csd.wustl.edu/Publications/Documents/RB13-09.pdf

Fagan, K. (2014, June 29). Salt Lake City a model for S.F. on homeless solutions. *SFGate.* Retrieved from http://www.sfgate.com/nation/article/Salt-Lake-City-a-model-for-S-F-on-homeless-5587357.php

Federal Deposit Insurance Corporation, Office of Inspector General. (2006, June). Challenges and FDIC efforts related to predatory lending. Report No. 06-011. Retrieved from https://www.fdicig.gov/reports06/06-011.pdf

Fincham, F. D., & Cain, K. M. (1986). Learned helplessness in humans: A developmental analysis. *Developmental Review, 6*(4), 301–333. doi:10.1016/0273-2297(86)90016-X

Flier, J. S. (2016, March 1). How to keep bad science from getting into print. *The Wall Street Journal.* Retrieved from http://www.wsj.com/articles/how-to-keep-bad-science-from-getting-into-print-1456874402

Freedman, S., Friedlander, D., Hamilton, G., Rock, J., Mitchell, M., Nudelman, J., ... Storto, L. (2000). Evaluating alternative welfare-to-work approaches: Two-year impacts for eleven programs. Manpower Demonstration Research Corporation. Retrieved from http://eric.ed.gov/?id=ED450276

Gallup. (2011). Healthways well-being index. Retrieved from http://www.well-beingindex.com

Godfrey, E. B., & Wolf, S. (2016). Developing critical consciousness or justifying the system? A qualitative analysis of attributions for poverty and wealth among low-income racial/ethnic minority and immigrant women. *Cultural Diversity and Ethnic Minority Psychology, 22*(1), 93–103. doi:10.1037/cdp0000048

Harnisch, T. L. (2010). Boosting financial literacy in America: A role for state colleges and universities. *Perspectives.* American Association of State Colleges and Universities. Retrieved from http://www.aascu.org/policy/publications/perspectives/financialliteracy.pdf

Holcomb, A. (2016, March 1). Mass incarceration and American drug laws [Letter to the editor]. *The Wall Street Journal.* Retrieved from http://www.wsj.com/articles/mass-incarceration-and-american-drug-laws-1456847599

Ianzito, C. (2015, December). The new face of hunger: Millions of older American struggle to get the right foods. *AARP Bulletin.* Retrieved from http://www.aarp.org/health/healthy-living/info-2015/hungry-seniors-health-nutrition.html

Ingraham, C. (2014, September 29). Our infant mortality rate is a national embarrassment. *The Washington Post.* Retrieved from https://www.washingtonpost.com/news/wonk/wp/2014/09/29/our-infant-mortality-rate-is-a-national-embarrassment/

Jemal, A., Thun, M. J., Ward, E. E., Henley, S. J., Cokkinides, V. E., and Murray, T. E. (2008). Mortality from leading causes by education and race in the United States, 2001. *American Journal of Preventive Medicine, 34*(1), 1–8. doi:http://dx.doi.org/10.1016/j.amepre.2007.09.017

Jiang, Y., Ekono, M., & Skinner, C. (2016, February). Basic facts about low-income children: Children under 18 years, 2014. National Center for Children in Poverty. Retrieved from http://www.nccp.org/publications/pub_1145.html

Jolin, M., Schmitz, P., & Seldon, W. (n.d.). Needle-moving community collaboratives: A promising approach to addressing America's biggest challenges. The Bridgespan Group. Retrieved from http://www.bridgespan.org/getmedia/7da1eafe-f85a-4798-8774-7386058f2ce4/needle-moving-community-collaboratives-report.aspx

Joint Commission on Accreditation of Healthcare Organizations (ed.). (1994). *Framework for improving performance: From principles to practice.* Oakbrook Terrace, IL: Joint Commission on Accreditation of Healthcare Organizations.

Jump$tart. (2013). Making the case for financial literacy—2013. http://jumpstart.org/assets/State-Sites/LA/files/downloads/Making-the-Case-2013.pdf

Kahle Research Solutions. (2012, September). Detroit safe community collaborative 'welcome home' initiative in the Osborn neighborhood [Mailing]. Available upon request from Kahle Research Solutions.

Kallenbach, L. R., & Smitherman, H. C. (2012, June). Dying before their time II. Retrieved from http://www.mi-seniors.net/pdfs/publications/Dying%20Before%20Their%20Time%20II%20-%20 2012%20Final%20Report.pdf

Kania, J., & Kramer, M. (2011, winter). Collective impact. *Stanford Social Innovation Review.* Retrieved from http://ssir.org/articles/entry/collective_impact

Karcher, M. (2015). Cross-age peer mentoring. *Research in Action, 7.* Retrieved from http://www.mentoring.org/new-site/wp-content/uploads/2015/09/RIA_ISSUE_7.pdf

Kennedy, B. (2015, February 18). America's 11 poorest cities. *CBS News.* Retrieved from http://www.cbsnews.com/media/americas-11-poorest-cities/

Kids Count Data Center. (2016a). Children in poverty (100 percent poverty). Annie E. Casey Foundation. Retrieved from http://datacenter.kidscount.org/data/tables/43-children-in-poverty-100-percent-poverty?loc=1&loct=1#detailed/1/any/false/869,36,868,867,133/any/321,322

Kids Count Data Center. (2016b). Population in poverty. Annie E. Casey Foundation. Retrieved from http://datacenter.kidscount.org/data/tables/52-population-in-poverty?loc=1&loct=1#detailed/1/any/false/869,36,868,867,133/any/339,340

Kiersz, A., & LoGiurato, B. (2015, June 18). Obama was right when he said 'this type of mass violence does not happen in other developed countries.' *Business Insider.* Retrieved from http://www.businessinsider.com/oecd-homicide-rates-chart-2015-6

Komisar, L. (1977). *Down and out in the USA: A history of public welfare* (Rev. ed.). New York, NY: New Viewpoints.

Koppelman, K., & Goodhart, R. L. (2008). Chapter 11. *Understanding human differences: Multicultural education for a diverse America* (2nd ed.). Boston, MA: Pearson. Retrieved from http://www.crosscultured.com/documents/C%20&%20A%20file/Classism0001.pdf

Lathrop, Y. M. (2014, February). Raising the minimum wage good for working families, good for Michigan's economy. Michigan League for Public Policy. Retrieved from http://www.mlpp.org/wp-content/uploads/2014/02/Raising-Minimum-Wage.pdf

Lee, S. (2014, May 13). Film examines health in relation to poverty. *New University.* Retrieved from http://www.newuniversity.org/2014/05/news/film-examines-health-in-relation-to-inequality/

Leonard, K. (2015, February 24). Medicaid enrollment surges across the U.S. *U.S. News & World Report.* Retrieved from http://www.usnews.com/news/articles/2015/02/24/medicaid-enrollment-surges-across-the-us

Lyons, A. C. (2007). Credit practices and financial education needs of Midwest college students [Working paper]. Networks Financial Institute at Indiana State University. Retrieved from http://www.usc.edu/dept/chepa/IDApays/publications/credit_practices.pdf

MacDorman, M. F., Mathews, T. J., Mohangoo, A. D., & Zeitlin, J. (2014). International comparisons of infant mortality and related factors: United States and Europe, 2010. National Vital Statistics Reports, 63(5). Retrieved from http://www.cdc.gov/nchs/data/nvsr/nvsr63/nvsr63_05.pdf

Matrix Human Services. (2013). A look inside the 'Transition To Success' program [Video]. YouTube. Retrieved from https://www.youtube.com/watch?v=eM_zGnZ0-tM

Matrix Human Services. (2016). 2014–2015 Matrix outcomes [mailing]. More information available upon request from www.matrixhumanservices.org

Michigan League for Public Policy. (2015). 2015 kids count in Michigan data book: Child well-being in Michigan, its counties and Detroit. Retrieved from http://www.mlpp.org/misc/KidsCount2015_FINAL_RGB_WEB.pdf

Michigan League for Public Policy. (2016). Kids count in Michigan data book 2016: Child well-being in Michigan, its counties and Detroit. Retrieved from http://www.mlpp.org/wp-content/uploads/2016/03/KC-11916-2016-Kids-Count-in-Michigan_final_web.pdf

Michigan's Campaign to End Homelessness. (1996). Homelessness in Michigan fact sheet. Retrieved from http://www.thecampaigntoendhomelessness.org/LinkClick.aspx?fileticket=PyAi7MFQN7o%3D&tabid=80&mid=429

Minnesota Housing Finance Agency. (n.d.). Self-sufficiency matrix. Retrieved from http://www.mnhousing.gov/get/MHFA_010996

Moeller, P. (2012, April 4). Why helping others makes us happy: Pursuing self-interested goals drives ongoing community engagement and raises self-esteem. U.S. News & World Report. Retrieved from http://money.usnews.com/money/personal-finance/articles/2012/04/04/why-helping-others-makes-us-happy

Muennig, P., Fiscella, K., Tancredi, D., & Franks, P. (2010). The relative health burden of selected social and behavioral risk factors in the United States: Implications for policy. *American Journal of Public Health, 100*(9), 1758–64. doi:10.2105/AJPH.2009.165019

National Center for Charitable Statistics. (n.d.). Quick facts about nonprofits. Retrieved from http://nccs.urban.org/statistics/quickfacts.cfm

Nolen, J. L. (2015). Learned helplessness. *Encyclopedia Britannica.* Retrieved from https://www.britannica.com/topic/learned-helplessness

Patterson, J. T. (1995). *America's struggle against poverty: 1900–1994.* Cambridge, MA: Harvard University Press.

Payne, R. K. (2013). *A framework for understanding poverty* (5th rev. ed.). Highlands, TX: aha! Process.

Peterson, C., Maier, S. F., & Seligman, M. E. P. (1993). *Learned helplessness: A theory for the age of personal control.* Oxford, England: Oxford University Press.

Piliavin, J. A., & Charng, H. W. (1990). Altruism: A review of recent theory and research. *Annual Review of Sociology, 16,* 27–65.

Post, S. (2005). Altruism, happiness, and health: It's good to be good. *International Journal of Behavioral Medicine, 12*(2), 66–77.

Professional guide to diseases (10th ed.). (2012). Professional Guide Series. Philadelphia, PA: Lippincott.

Radawski, D. (1999). Continuous quality improvement: Origins, concepts, problems and applications. *Perspective on Physician Education, 10*(1), 12–16. Retrieved from http://www2.paeaonline.org/index.php?ht=action/GetDocumentAction/i/25258?

Robbins, T., Stagman, S., & Smith, S. (2012, October). Young children at risk: National and state prevalence of risk factors. National Center for Children in Poverty. Retrieved from http://www.nccp.org/publications/pdf/text_1073.pdf

Robert Wood Johnson Foundation. (2011, December). Health care's blind side: The overlooked connection between social needs and good health.

Schwartz, B. (2014, February 11). Re-entry programs and recidivism: The connection. The Lionheart Foundation. Retrieved from http://lionheart.org/guest-blog-re-entry-programs-recidivism-the-connection/

Shaefer, L., & Edin, K. (2014, Summer). The rise of extreme poverty in the United States. *Pathways.* Retrieved from http://inequality.stanford.edu/_media/pdf/pathways/summer_2014/Pathways_Summer_2014_ShaeferEdin.pdf

Stuber, J., & Kronebusch, K. (2004). Stigma and other determinants of participation in TANF and Medicaid. *Journal of Policy Analysis Management, 23*(3), 509–30. doi: 10.1002/pam.20024

Stuber, J., & Schlesinger, M. (2006). Sources of stigma for means-tested government programs. *Social Science and Medicine, 63*(4):933–45. doi:10.1016/j.socscimed.2006.01.012

Surowiecki, J. (2014, September 22). Give the homeless homes. *The New Yorker.* Retrieved from http://www.newyorker.com/magazine/2014/09/22/home-free

Swanson, A. (2015, April 9). How the U.S. spends more helping its citizens than other rich countries, but gets way less. *The Washington Post.* Retrieved from https://www.washingtonpost.com/news/wonk/wp/2015/04/09/how-the-u-s-spends-more-helping-its-citizens-than-other-rich-countries-but-gets-way-less/

United Ways of Michigan. (2014, September). ALICE Michigan: Study of financial hardship. Retrieved from http://www.unitedwayalice.org/documents/14UW%20ALICE%20Report_MI_Lowres_10.24.15.pdf

U.S. Census Bureau. (2016). Poverty. Retrieved from http://www.census.gov/topics/income-poverty/poverty.html

U.S. Office of Management and Budget. (2013). Fiscal year 2013 historical tables. Retrieved from https://www.whitehouse.gov/sites/default/files/omb/budget/fy2013/assets/hist.pdf

Wessler, S. (2009). Race and recession: How inequality rigged the socio-economy and how to change the rules. Applied Research Center. Retrieved from https://www.raceforward.org/sites/default/files/downloads/2009_race_recession_0909.pdf

Woltman, E., Grogan-Kaylor, A., Perron, B., Georges, H., Kilbourne, A . M., & Bauer, M. S. (2012). Comparative effectiveness of collaborative chronic care models for mental health conditions across primary, specialty, and behavioral health care settings: Systematic review and meta-analysis. *American Journal of Psychiatry, 169*(8), 790–804. doi:10.1176/appi.ajp.2012.11111616

Woodruff, M. (2015, February 10). The $46 billion payday lending industry is in for a big blow. Retrieved from http://finance.yahoo.com/news/CFPB-payday-lending-rules-explained-192558796.html

World Health Organization. (2016). Social determinants of health: What are social determinants of health? Retrieved from http://www.who.int/social_determinants/sdh_definition/en/

WE'D LIKE TO HEAR FROM YOU!

aha!
Process, Inc.
A Ruby Payne Company

Join us on Facebook
www.facebook.com/rubypayne
www.facebook.com/ahaprocess

Twitter
www.twitter.com/ahaprocess
#PovertyChat
#BridgesOutofPoverty

Pinterest
www.pinterest.com/ahaprocess

Subscribe to our YouTube channel
www.youtube.com/ahaprocess

Respond to our blog
www.ahaprocess.com/blog

Download free resources
www.ahaprocess.com